Cambridge Elements ≡

Elements in Politics and Society in Latin America
edited by
Maria Victoria Murillo
Columbia University
Tulia G. Falleti
University of Pennsylvania
Juan Pablo Luna
The Pontifical Catholic University of Chile
Andrew Schrank
Brown University

THE INDIGENOUS RIGHT TO SELF-DETERMINATION IN EXTRACTIVIST ECONOMIES

Marcela Torres-Wong
Latin American Faculty of Social Sciences

CAMBRIDGE
UNIVERSITY PRESS

Shaftesbury Road, Cambridge CB2 8EA, United Kingdom

One Liberty Plaza, 20th Floor, New York, NY 10006, USA

477 Williamstown Road, Port Melbourne, VIC 3207, Australia

314–321, 3rd Floor, Plot 3, Splendor Forum, Jasola District Centre,
New Delhi – 110025, India

103 Penang Road, #05–06/07, Visioncrest Commercial, Singapore 238467

Cambridge University Press is part of Cambridge University Press & Assessment,
a department of the University of Cambridge.

We share the University's mission to contribute to society through the pursuit of
education, learning and research at the highest international levels of excellence.

www.cambridge.org
Information on this title: www.cambridge.org/9781009410908

DOI: 10.1017/9781009410861

First published 2023

A catalogue record for this publication is available from the British Library.

ISBN 978-1-009-41090-8 Paperback
ISSN 2515-5253 (online)
ISSN 2515-5245 (print)

Cambridge University Press & Assessment has no responsibility for the persistence
or accuracy of URLs for external or third-party internet websites referred to in this
publication and does not guarantee that any content on such websites is, or will
remain, accurate or appropriate.

The Indigenous Right to Self-Determination in Extractivist Economies

Elements in Politics and Society in Latin America

DOI: 10.1017/9781009410861
First published online: May 2023

Marcela Torres-Wong
Latin American Faculty of Social Sciences
Author for correspondence: Marcela Torres-Wong, marcela.torres@flacso .edu.mx

Abstract: International norms widely recognize the Indigenous right to self-determination by which Indigenous peoples define and pursue their collective aspirations. Nevertheless, as progressive as legal frameworks might appear, in reality few Indigenous communities enjoy this right and most remain vulnerable and disempowered. Activists blame Latin America's extractivist economies, while governments argue that extractive revenues are necessary to improve Indigenous life. Far from presenting a unified position, rural Indigenous peoples are most often divided over extractive industries. To assess how Indigenous self-determination has progressed, and the role that extractivism plays in this, this Element examines six Indigenous communities in Mexico, Bolivia, and Peru with contrasting experiences of extractive projects. It finds that the Indigenous ability to use favorable legislation in conjunction with available economic resources shapes different self-determination outcomes. Finally, it assesses Indigenous possibilities for self-determination in the light of environmental activism and discourses on *Buen Vivir*.

This Element also has a video abstract: Cambridge.org/The Indigenous Right to Self-Determination in Extractivist Economies_Torres-Wong
Keywords: Indigenous, communities, self-determination, extractivism, environmentalism

ISBNs: 9781009410908 (PB), 9781009410861 (OC)
ISSNs: 2515-5253 (online), 2515-5245 (print)

Contents

1 Introduction

In 2020, Santiago Manuin, a Peruvian Indigenous leader and activist, died of COVID-19 in a hospital in Chiclayo city hundreds of miles from his hometown of Santa Maria de Nieva, an Indigenous locality in the Amazonas region. After fighting the disease for several days, Santiago was transferred from a hospital in the city of Bagua that had limited medical capabilities in order to obtain adequate treatment. His son declared to the press that his father had died due to the indifference of the state: "it is sad to see Amazonian people die in the very lungs of the planet due to the lack of oxygen" (Modino 2020). Like Santiago, thousands of Indigenous peoples in Latin America have lost their lives due to inadequate medical care (Cepal 2020).

In 2009, Santiago Manuin led the *Baguazo* protest against attempts by Alan García, then president of Peru, to promote hydrocarbon extraction in Amazonia; he was shot and wounded, but survived the attack. Manuin believed that Indigenous communities should not become the allies of extractive companies in exchange for profit. He dedicated much of his life to searching for alternative funding to bring health care and education to his people (Servindi 2015). Today, more than half of Latin America's Indigenous populations have migrated to urban areas in search of better living conditions, yet they are subject to discrimination and likely to have low-paid jobs (World Bank 2013). Meanwhile, those peoples still living in rural communities face the dilemma of rejecting a state that imposes a development model that differs from their own or accepting the model in exchange for resources to cope with the multiple adversities they face on a daily basis (Henriksen 2001). Extractivism is a defining feature of this model, which depends on the expansion of natural resource exploitation as a key driver of national economic growth (Svampa 2019; Gudynas 2015).

In Latin America, both left- and right-leaning governments promote extractive industries at the expense of Indigenous natural environments (Svampa 2019; Gouritin 2018; Veltmeyer and Petras 2014). Extractivist economies are organized around the maximization of revenue through the extraction and exportation of commodities (Durante et al. 2021). Large-scale mining, oil and gas drilling, dams, highways, waterways, and, more recently, renewable energy industries and agrobusiness jeopardize the livelihoods of Indigenous communities all across the subcontinent (Animal Político 2020; Svampa 2019; Anaya 2010). Against this backdrop, COVID-19 is just another threat that Indigenous communities must face, together with alarming poverty, climate vulnerability, criminalization, and violence (Global Witness 2020; International Labour Organization 2020).

Santiago Manuin's life is one example of the harsh conditions under which Indigenous leaders must operate in the fight for their rights. These conditions taint the enthusiasm of activists and scholars for the victories secured by the transnational Indigenous movement ensuring the recognition of their right to self-determine their collective future (Lightfoot 2016). The adoption of International Labour Organization (ILO) Convention 169 in 1989 was a watershed for policies typically used by national governments to address Indigenous rights. In contrast with integrationist approaches, the ILO recognized a wide range of rights based upon the Indigenous condition of peoples entitled to the protection of their territories, cultural identities, religions, and political institutions. In 2007, the United Nations' Declaration on the Rights of Indigenous Peoples (UNDRIP) explicitly incorporated the right to self-determination which had been denied by several countries. By virtue of this right, Indigenous populations can freely determine their political status and pursue their economic, social, and cultural development. The Declaration also states that in exercising this right, they may enjoy autonomy or self-government in matters relating to their internal and local affairs, as well as regarding the ways and means of financing their autonomous functions (United Nations 2007, Articles 3 and 4). In 2016, the Organization of American States (OAS) also recognized self-determination in the American Declaration on the Rights of Indigenous Peoples (Article III of OAS Declaration; see OAS [2016]).

In reaction to international recognition of Indigenous rights, legal scholars, anthropologists, and political ecologists have produced an extensive literature documenting how Indigenous rights are persistently violated by governments and extractive companies in Latin America and elsewhere in the postcolonial world (Scheidel et al. 2020; Gutiérrez and Del Pozo 2019; Gouritin 2018; Temper et al. 2015). However, few studies analyze comparatively how disenfranchised Indigenous communities can take ownership of extant legal frameworks and available resources to actually improve life in their territories. This Element aims to fill that void.

So how can Indigenous peoples in countries where extractivism prevails exercise their right to self-determination? During the 1990s and guided by the spirit of ILO Convention 169, many Latin American governments introduced constitutional reforms that recognized the multicultural composition of their countries and emphasized the rights of Indigenous peoples.[1] Increasing Indigenous claims for collective rights also prompted some governments to pass specific legislation enabling Indigenous peoples to use their customary law

---

[1] Multiculturalism attempted to solve the problem of discrimination against minorities by recognizing these groups' rights to be treated as distinctive peoples entitled to collective as well as individual rights (Kymlicka 1995).

to elect representatives, administer justice according to their cultural values, and use their political institutions to administer their lands and resources, among other rights (Lucero 2013; Van Cott 2006). However, even when governments have recognized rights on paper, most neither created regulations nor distributed the necessary resources to implement these rights (Burguette 2013; Martínez Novo 2013; Hale 2002).

Several anthropologists studying Latin American Indigenous movements have concluded that multicultural reforms were functional for neoliberal policies. These scholars emphasize that while Indigenous cultural rights were legally recognized these reforms did not address structural inequalities, which carried the risk of demobilizing Indigenous movements (Gustafson 2009; Hale 2002; Povinelli 2002; Tapia 2000; Wade 1997). As these scholars suggest, the lack of economic resources prevents Indigenous leaders from creating autonomous development models to improve life in their communities.

During the 1990s and early 2000s, unprecedented waves of Indigenous mobilization, in opposition to neoliberal policies, broke into national and international political arenas (Martí Puig 2010). Hundreds of Indigenous activists claimed that the privatization of community lands for the advancement of extractive companies was destroying the natural environment upon which Indigenous communities depended to survive. Drawing upon the work of the ILO, Indigenous movements demanded the right to be consulted about any project implemented on their territories. Alliances with international NGOs and environmental activists enabled Indigenous organizations to form transnational networks united around a powerful political discourse connecting Indigenous rights with the protection of Mother Earth (Pieck 2006, Pacheco-Vega 2006).

In the Andean countries, new political actors built upon Indigenous movements' discourses to criticize neoliberal policies. With the support of Indigenous voters, leftist governments in Bolivia (2006), Ecuador (2007), and – with less intensity – Peru (2011) came to power promising to respect Indigenous rights. In these three countries, governments delivered on their campaign commitments either through constitutional recognition of the right to prior consultation or through legislation addressing this right. Simultaneously, however, the promotion of extractive industries remained central for national economies, although in Bolivia and Ecuador the state took a more prominent lead than in Peru (Gudynas 2012).

Prior consultation has gradually extended to the rest of Latin America, becoming the model that shapes state–Indigenous relations (Flemmer and Schilling-Vacaflor 2016). Ideally, prior consultation guarantees Indigenous self-determination by preventing imposition by states or private companies. However, scholars studying consultations agree that a significant limitation of these procedures is that national governments are not willing to accept opposition to extractive industries (Gustafsson and Schilling-Vacaflor 2022; Torres-Wong 2019; Flemmer and Schilling-Vacaflor 2016). Prior consultations with Latin America's Indigenous peoples generally result in acceptance of projects (Guarneros-Meza and Zaremberg 2019; Torres-Wong 2019). Governments exploit Indigenous political weakness, internal disagreement, territorial fragmentation, and critical economic situations to obtain approval of ecologically controversial projects (Rodríguez-Garavito 2011; Zaremberg and Torres-Wong 2018). In the best-case scenario, prior consultations serve to negotiate compensation in exchange for allowing extraction. Yet, many of these communities perceive the trade-off between a loss of their culture and access to economic resources as unfair (Gustafsson and Schilling-Vacaflor 2022). Nevertheless, most Indigenous representatives end up agreeing to participate in such projects as they suspect that these will proceed anyway, with or without their consent.

Both the first wave of rights recognition in the 1990s and the second wave beginning in the mid-2000s had unsatisfactory results for Indigenous communities. However, over the past two decades Latin American countries have experienced significant economic growth derived, to a large extent, from the commodity boom (2000–2014). In the context of regional economic growth, more economic resources became available for those Indigenous communities willing to comply with extractivism. While the first wave of multicultural rights remained rhetorical, predominately emphasizing folkloric aspects of Indigenous cultures, the second wave consisted of formal consultation procedures with Indigenous representatives and economic compensation for extractive activities. Nonetheless, the risks of environmental destruction are ever-present (Leifsen et al. 2017). Environmentalists quickly turned against national governments and extractive companies, accusing them of using bribes to divide Indigenous communities.

Indigenous peoples typically organize into international, national, and subnational political organizations. At the local level they are frequently organized in federations, cooperatives, unions, or captaincies, comprising various communities that share a common history and territory (Stavenhagen 2010:35). While the discourse of Indigenous organizations at the international and national levels generally presents a unified position against the extractive industry, within Indigenous territories communities remain divided over negotiating with extractive companies. Some communities reject extractive projects as they believe that the materialization of their rights should be pursued without compromising the integrity of their territories. Other communities argue that the use of extractive revenues to improve their living conditions is legitimate (Arce 2014; Arellano-Yanguas 2011).

In this Element, I compare six Indigenous communities that inhabit six rural municipalities in Mexico (Figure 1), Peru (Figure 2), and Bolivia (Figure 3): Capulálpam de Méndez (Mexico), Homún (Mexico), Oxiacaque (Mexico),

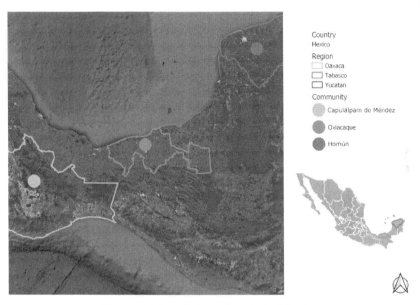

Figure 1 Map of sites of study in Mexico

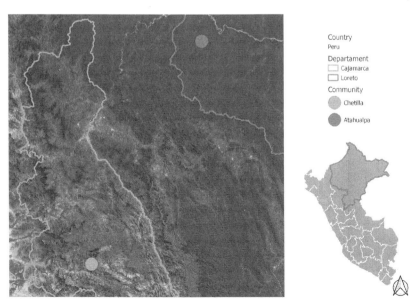

Figure 2 Map of sites of study in Peru

Figure 3 Map of site of study in Bolivia

Chetilla (Peru), Atahualpa (Peru), and Ingre (Bolivia). In these communities, the ability of local leaders to use favorable legislation to their benefit differs, as does the type of economic resources available to them to improve community life.

Based on these cases, I propose the following theory: the interaction between (1) Indigenous use of favorable legal frameworks (electoral autonomy regimes, justice administration, customary laws, prior consultation, compensation mechanisms), and (2) the available economic resources for Indigenous communities (extractive resources, nonextractive resources, or none), shape Indigenous self-determination outcomes (I develop this further in Section 2). An important lesson emerging from the cases is that Indigenous leaders generally agree that economic resources – either extractive or nonextractive – are needed to improve Indigenous life. Local economies in the form of agriculture, cattle raising, fishing, and ecotourism are some of the preferred economic activities within Indigenous communities. According to the leaders interviewed for this project, the exercise of self-determination should include the sustainable use of natural resources, though this is not an option for everyone.

1.1 Why Study Indigenous Communities?

I argue that Indigenous communities living in rural municipalities are caught between two extremes. At one end of the spectrum are the Indigenous populations living in voluntary isolation or extreme autonomous groups, such as the

Zapatistas in Chiapas, who choose to live independently, outside of state law and without depending on state resources. While these types of communities tend to receive much press coverage, they remain the minority. At the other extreme are the vast majority of Indigenous peoples who migrate to the cities, seeking to improve their lives.

Rural Indigenous communities comprise a large proportion of the Indigenous population that is struggling for self-determination within the boundaries of nation-states.[2] For these communities, self-determination is not incompatible with the administrative organization of the state. From the outset, modern Indigenous political organizations have been defined by interactions between Indigenous normative systems and state laws (Sieder 2019). These interactions are largely a consequence of violent colonial imposition, which is why there is a demand for self-determination. However, complete autonomy is improbable for most Indigenous communities.

In contrast to the few empirical studies on Indigenous self-determination that focus on the efforts of subnational Indigenous political organizations to create autonomous governments (Merino 2020; Sieder 2017), I argue that self-determination is experienced more intensely within rural municipalities. By only examining the actions of supra–community organizations and their impact on national politics, political scientists may overlook the gap between the political goals of these organizations and the diverse realities of Indigenous communities that inhabit Latin America's most biodiverse and resource-rich territories. Most Indigenous leaders operating at the community level direct their political efforts at obtaining state resources for community projects. Typically, these resources are channeled and distributed by municipal governments, which explains why many community leaders still seek to have a stake in this branch of the state rather than rejecting it to form autonomous Indigenous entities.

There is much to be learned about the daily struggles of rural Indigenous leaders seeking to improve Indigenous living conditions without assimilating into mainstream societies. We know that Indigenous access to economic resources is urgent due to the extreme poverty and climate vulnerability of rural regions (Anaya 2010; Stavenhagen 2007; Graham 2004). Most Indigenous leaders face significant obstacles to maintaining their political institutions, let alone being able to implement projects that can reduce Indigenous vulnerability.

---

[2] Unlike rural Indigenous movements, urban Indigenous struggles are deterritorialized. Indigenous migrants use ethnicity strategically in their interactions with state institutions to demand their right to live in the cities with full access to housing, education, health care, and jobs (Herrera Amaya 2018).

By examining how self-determination unfolds at the community level, I follow Donna Lee Van Cott's suggestion for enhancing our understanding of ordinary Indigenous politics (Van Cott 2010). I propose a shift in focus away from the influence of Indigenous politics *on* national politics and toward the impact that the interaction between Indigenous use of favorable legislation and available economic resources has on the realization of Indigenous rights within rural communities.

1.2 Outline of the Element

This Element makes three important contributions to our understanding of Indigenous politics in Latin America. First, it reveals the progress that has been made in the last thirty years regarding the rights of some of the most disempowered populations in the region. The presence of extractive companies in Indigenous territories often divides Indigenous communities and polarizes debates over Indigenous rights. By comparing pro-extractivist and anti-extractivist Indigenous communities, I attempt to go beyond existing divisions over whether the mere acceptance of extractivism precludes self-determination. Furthermore, I focus on the paths that are currently most available to Indigenous communities living in extractivist national contexts. Second, the empirical analysis identifies two factors whose interaction is underexplored in the literature: Indigenous use of favorable legal frameworks and economic resources available for the realization of Indigenous rights. The study highlights how these two factors interact and shape Indigenous self-determination outcomes. Third, my analysis reveals the pragmatic use of available laws and resources by rural Indigenous leaders to achieve community goals, rather than the idealized versions disseminated in international forums. I also emphasize the concern of most of these leaders to preserve the integrity of their environments and the limited options they have within extractivist settings.

In Section 2, I present the theory derived from case analysis. I then discuss the argument, methodology, case selection, and scholarly work on the subject. In Section 3, I conduct a comparison of six cases in Bolivia, Peru, and Mexico and create a typology for self-determination outcomes. I then show how the different self-determination outcomes found in the cases align – or not – with the goals of environmental activists and Indigenous discourses on *Buen Vivir* ("good living"). In the Conclusion, I summarize my findings and highlight their implications for a better understanding of Indigenous communities and the complex paths through which self-determination can be achieved.

2 Theory and Methods

The proposed theory was developed inductively as it stems from the analysis of the six cases examined in this Element. I argue that different self-determination outcomes are shaped by the interaction between the use that Indigenous leaders make of existing legal frameworks and the economic resources available for Indigenous communities. The theory contains preliminary hypotheses to provide readers with new analytical frameworks with which to assess Indigenous struggles for self-determination. The purpose of the study is not to establish causal explanations for the variation between Indigenous communities, but to identify similarities and differences related to the two factors outlined above that allow us to understand the diverse trajectories experienced by these six communities from Bolivia, Peru, and Mexico.

In Section 2.1, I first define self-determination by drawing upon public statements by Indigenous leaders from different Latin American countries, together with legal definitions contained in international laws. Second, I discuss whether Indigenous self-determination is compatible with extractive industries and conclude that the exercise of this right entails a process that goes beyond decisions over extractive projects. I then formulate my preliminary hypotheses drawing upon my findings and the extant research on the topic. Finally, I introduce the comparative methodology used to identify and analyze similarities and differences across the cases.

2.1 Self-Determination in Theory and Practice

In 2007, the United Nations (UN) upheld the claim of Indigenous national and international organizations from across the postcolonial world by explicitly including the right to self-determination in the UNDRIP. According to Articles 3 and 4 of this declaration, Indigenous peoples are granted the right to freely determine their political status and to freely pursue their economic, social, and cultural development. The declaration adds that in exercising self-determination, "Indigenous peoples have the right to *autonomy or self-government* in matters relating to their internal and local affairs, *as well as ways and means for financing their autonomous functions*" (United Nations 2007, Article 4, emphasis added).

With this inclusion, the UN sought to remedy the omission made by ILO Convention 169 (1989). Despite breaking with the integrationist model under which the international community had addressed Indigenous rights, the ILO heeded the objections made by various governments which, in 1984, argued against Indigenous self-determination, expressing concern for sovereignty and national integrity (Lightfoot 2009:101). In 2016, OAS also included this right in

Article 3 of the American Declaration on the Rights of Indigenous Peoples (Cerqueira 2020).

In order to safeguard the interests of nation-states, both instruments address the internal dimension of self-determination by which different peoples around the world may decide their political and economic status within the political frameworks of their countries. In this regard, Article 46 (1) of UNDRIP states that: "nothing in the declaration may be interpreted ... or construed as authorizing or encouraging any action which would dismember or impair, totally or in part, the territorial integrity or political unity of sovereign and independent States" (for more details see Article 46 of the UNDRIP [United Nations 2007:28]). It has been argued that this limits Indigenous rights; however, these voices are a minority among the many more who have enthusiastically celebrated the declaration (Lightfoot 2021).

2.2 Self-Determination as Defined by Indigenous Voices

In the early 1990s, Indigenous movements in Mexico, Guatemala, Chile, Ecuador, Bolivia, and the Amazonian basin appeared on the national and international political scene demanding the right to rule their territories and freely determine their future (Martí Puig 2010). Nourished by the spirit of ILO Convention 169, Indigenous political organizations at different levels clamored for their right to govern their land and people according to their customary laws and political institutions. Most Latin American governments responded to these claims, at least superficially, by granting different forms of collective rights.

With the advancement of extractive industries deeper into rural areas, the right to self-determination took on a more defensive slant. National, international, and subnational Indigenous political organizations focused their struggle on the right to decide on the use of Indigenous territories. In the streets and in the courts, the right to prior consultation introduced by ILO Convention 169 became the emblematic tool with which to achieve territorial self-determination. Indigenous activists and their NGO supporters litigated various cases and won as national and international courts halted projects for failing to consult with Indigenous communities. Scholars examining these legal gains acknowledge the opportunities gained by Indigenous peoples in having a say in matters concerning their territories (Wright and Tomaselli 2020). As governments began to carry out prior consultations, however, and to secure Indigenous approval in most cases, other academics have expressed concern about the negative consequences of making prior consultation the core of Indigenous activism (Gómez Rivera 2013).

More recently, legal scholars and activists have recaptured the spirit of Indigenous rights, by shifting the focus back to the content of self-determination. In March 2021, the Due Process of Law Foundation, Oxfam, and Fundar released a report entitled "The Right to Self-determination of Indigenous Peoples in Mexico" ("La Libre Determinación de los Pueblos Indígenas en México") (Ramírez Espinosa and Cerqueira 2021). Among other things, the authors compile various experiences detailing the obstacles to the realization of this right. More importantly, the report includes the testimonies of several Indigenous representatives that define the content of self-determination. I use some of these testimonies, together with others from Indigenous leaders across Latin America, to identify patterns across definitions. Some definitions provided by Indigenous leaders and Indigenous political organizations are cited below.[3]

For Maria de los Angeles Santiago Sánchez, an Indigenous member of San Antonino Castillo Velasco in Ocotlán, Oaxaca: "self-determination means that we *use the ways of working of our communities*; *elect the people that will represent us in the municipalities, decide what happens in our territories, and decide what is best for the community* including the participation of all" (Ramírez Espinosa and Cerqueira 2021, emphasis added).

For Vicente Ferreira, an Indigenous leader from El Chaco, Bolivia: "self-determination is the possibility to *define our destiny*, [about] how to *manage development*, and to *accept the projects* we want and *reject* those we do not want" (personal communication January 14, 2021, emphasis added).

The National Confederation of Indigenous Nationalities from Ecuador (CONAIE) defines self-determination as: "Indigenous peoples *making decisions* about *our development*, *management of lands and natural resources*, preserving *our traditional forms of social organizing* and *self-*government, specially over *education, health care, justice administration and political institutions*" (CONAIE 2012, emphasis added).

On June 22, 2020, in a virtual panel on Autonomy, Self-Determination, and Decolonization organized by Servindi, a civil society organization working in intercultural communication, Atencio López Martínez, who belongs to the Kuna people from Panama, argued that: "Self-determination is not a dream anymore … it is a reality. *Against economic and political impositions*, Indigenous peoples have rights. We have *history*, we have *territory*, we have *sovereignty*" (Servindi 2020, emphasis added).

During the same event, Mexican Indigenous leader María de Jesús Patricia Martínez, internationally known as Marichuy, said:

---

[3] All translations from Spanish to English of interviewees quoted are my own.

> Our Zapatista brothers, they have their caracoles, their juntas de *Buen Gobierno* [Good Government Boards], they have *their own municipalities*, they use *their own laws* and *do not use public funds*. Also, other brothers from Cherán ... *gained autonomy within the same municipal structures*. Also, in Guerrero, they have *their own community police*. They are *organized to protect* themselves ... also the *use of traditional medicine is an exercise of autonomy*. Megaprojects jeopardize this autonomy. Then *it is not just self-government but also protecting our territories*. (Servindi 2020, emphasis added)

Santiago Jesús Manuin, a young Amazonia leader, son of the Peruvian Indigenous leader Santiago Manuin said:

> The state always denied our right to self-determination. My father together with other leaders undertook a process of articulation with the state to let them know *we had to organize* and become an *autonomous territory, with our education system, also our own medicine, our territory,* while *still being Peruvians.* . . . Peru is a plurinational state ... [and] that should mean that we can exercise our rights according *to our customary law, as stated by international law.* (Centro Amázonico de Antropología Aplicada 2020, emphasis added)

Finally, in the words of the Indigenous leader from the community of San Felipe de los Herreros in Michoacan: "According to the right of self-determination, Indigenous communities *elect their authorities* to *govern* their territories. They can *organize* according to their *customary norms*. Indigenous communities have rights *to autonomy and self-government*. If they *use public resources*, they must follow legal frameworks regarding transparency, fiscal inspection, and administrative responsibility" (Ramírez Espinosa and Cerqueira 2021:83, emphasis added).

All these definitions reflect Indigenous diversity. However, they also share common features: election of representatives; use of customary norms to organize community life; territorial protection; decision-making; and control of lands, resources, development, health, and education. Accordingly, Ramírez Espinosa and Cerqueira propose a broad definition of self-determination as the opportunity to build a community life project according to the will of Indigenous community members that entails autonomy; self-identification; access to land, territory, and natural resources; cultural integrity; to be consulted about and freely consent to any measures that impact Indigenous livelihoods; to rule and be ruled according to Indigenous laws; to elect representatives using cultural traditions; and to decide development models (Ramírez Espinosa and Cerqueira 2021:15).

As various anthropologists suggest, Indigenous territories are constitutive of self-determination (Martínez et al. 2018; Díaz Polanco 1997). Accordingly, the Indigenous definitions cited above address general aspects of how life in these territories should be organized. Self-determination can take a variety of forms as diverse as Indigenous communities themselves, their history, and their aspirations. However, there are several intertwined objectives that emerge from Indigenous public declarations and testimonies. I develop this further in the following section.

2.3 The Multidimensional Nature of Self-Determination

Self-determination is a complex process encompassing multiple dimensions of Indigenous well-being (Ndayambaje and Fulgence 2017; Flemmer and Schilling-Vacaflor 2016; Lightfoot 2016; Cornell 2006). In the words of James Anaya, former UN Special Rapporteur on the rights of Indigenous peoples, substantive self-determination includes the right to make meaningful choices in matters that touch upon all spheres of life on a continuous basis, such as economic, cultural, and social development (Anaya 2000). This is consistent with the Indigenous testimonies detailed in Section 2.2, which provide holistic definitions of self-determination by linking it with multiple aspects of community life.

First, a political dimension, overemphasized in the last twenty years with the increase of extractive projects, relates to the right to decide on the use of Indigenous territories. As such, disputes between Indigenous communities and national governments have centered on who controls land and the subsoil resources underneath Indigenous lands (Picq 2020). Prior consultation is the mechanism designed by international legislators to decentralize decision-making from national governments to Indigenous communities, although with limited results.

Second, a cultural dimension is repeatedly emphasized by Indigenous political organizations and their legal advocates and is also present in the Indigenous definitions detailed in Section 2.2. Culture, however, is not easy to define. Millions of people across the world self-identify as Indigenous and demand their right to live according to their traditions. Legal definitions of Indigenous cultures generally relate to ancestral practices based on specific systems of belief, defined locally and temporally (e.g. Ley para la Protección de los Derechos de la Comunidad Maya del Estado de Yucatán, 2011 [Law for the Protection of the Rights of Maya Communities in Yucatán]). Conversely, more dynamic notions of Indigenous cultural identities understand these as fluid and relational, and not defined by immutable essences or historic ties to the past (Guevara 2009; Hale and Millamán 2007). Many Indigenous leaders and community members constantly interact with the mestizo society, state officials, religious institutions, or NGO activists. Some Indigenous communities have coexisted with foreign and national companies operating on their lands for decades, while many other Indigenous members temporally or permanently migrate to cities in search of economic opportunities. In these interactions, distinctive cultural markers such as language, religious beliefs, and customary norms are either lost or adjusted in order to be preserved.

For Hale and Millamán (2007), cultural resistance forges political unity and builds the trenches from which effective political challenges can occur. Against this backdrop, culture is better understood as ongoing dynamics of resistance, adaptation, and recreation performed by Indigenous peoples from the position of social exclusion that they have occupied since colonial times (Guevara 2009:91). Culture is not located at the level of the individual nor at that of a reified society, but at the intersubjective level where it provides a means for identifying group boundaries, interpreting events, and according value (Della Porta and Keating 2008:9). Culture informs and legitimizes conceptions of self, of social and political organization, of how the world works, and how the individual and group function in the world (Graham 2004). As such, culture is not solely ancestral nor static; rather, it entails a permanent process of recuperation, change, and adaptation.

Based on the studies mentioned, I argue that the cultural dimension of self-determination manifests through community-based practices and narratives that infuse a collective dimension of belonging. Community assemblies, community work, and traditions, among others, are typical manifestations of Indigenous cultural values. Also, new traditions that recreate Indigenous history, such as the performance of *autoconsultas* (self-consultations) used to replace prior consultations, or the renewal of Indigenous myths to attract tourists and improve local economies, are examples of cultural dynamism. These practices reflect the will of community members to perpetuate their existence as Indigenous peoples by resisting assimilation and enabling collective survival.

Third, there is an economic dimension related to the Indigenous right to self-determine their development (Article 32 of UNDRIP). Various legal scholars argue that self-determination relates to the survival of Indigenous cultures as much as it relates to strengthening Indigenous economies (Oliva and Blázquez 2007:246; Cornell 2006 cited by Figuera Vargas and Ariza Lascarro 2015). According to this understanding, the exercise of self-determination should enable Indigenous peoples to maintain and strengthen their local institutions and build upon them to develop strong economic models (Graham 2004). This economic understanding of self-determination is coherent with Indigenous definitions emphasizing the right to manage development, lands, and natural resources for community well-being, and to use public resources or accept only the projects they want, in their best interests. Such views on economy oppose states' historical impositions of economic projects that have endangered Indigenous livelihoods. The economic dimension of self-determination is also laid down in Article 4 of UNDRIP, which states that Indigenous peoples should have the means to finance their autonomous functions (United Nations 2007, Article 4).

Fourth, a legal dimension of self-determination is expressed through Indigenous demands to rule and be ruled according to their own normative systems or customary laws. Historically, colonial and racist empires, and later states, treated Indigenous peoples as uncivilized groups forced to abide by the different legal frameworks regulating the complex functioning of national states. This was changed by ILO 169 and other international norms that followed. However, although states have incorporated political and legal reforms validating Indigenous laws, national legal systems are slow to change and Indigenous political organizations continue to defend their normative systems as more appropriate for solving problems and regulating life in their communities. Mechanisms to elect authorities, solve conflicts, carry out economic transactions, administer lands and natural resources, adopt political decisions, and control criminal activities are part of Indigenous legal traditions.

As legal pluralism scholars have extensively argued, Indigenous laws are neither immutable nor completely independent of state laws or other legal systems (Starr and Collier 2018; Guevera-Gil and Thome 1992; Albó 1987). Indigenous leaders may sometimes reject the imposition more than the content of state regulations. The legal dimension of self-determination implies the Indigenous right to be ruled by laws that have legitimacy and are culturally appropriate for Indigenous communities. These laws can, however, change and adjust over time as communities develop new ways of regulating their lives.

All the dimensions detailed – political, cultural, economic, and legal – are, in some way, contained in two concepts that Indigenous political organizations repeatedly stress and which international norms include in their definition of self-determination: autonomy and self-government (González et al. 2021). These concepts are intertwined and sometimes used interchangeably by scholars and activists. However, I propose an analytical distinction between the two concepts that has emerged from my case analysis and that may be useful for further studies on self-determination.

In the literature on social movements, autonomy is defined as the capacity of social organizations to implement political projects without being incorporated into the state. In this view, the state represents an ever-present risk of cooptation and demobilization (Cortés 2008, cited by Zaremberg and Guzmán 2019). Applied to the case of Indigenous movements striving for validation of their political organization and use of their territories and resources, autonomy

Table 1. Self-determination Dimensions

SELF-DETERMINATION	DIMENSIONS	EMPIRCAL EVIDENCE
AUTONOMY	Political	Community leaders can veto unwanted state projects, policies or regulations impacting Indigenous territories.
	Economic	Community leaders can undertake economic projects in their community to create wellbeing among members.
SELF-GOVERNMENT	Legal	Customary laws regulate internal affairs in the community (election of authorities, conflict solutions, land and resource affairs)
	Cultural	Cultural practices (community assemblies, community work, cultural beliefs and traditions) are part of life in the community.

entails Indigenous ability to decide which political and economic paths to follow, rather than accepting development models from above. Self-government, on the other hand, while deeply connected with autonomy, relates to the Indigenous ability to be ruled by their own normative systems and choose their authorities according to their cultural values and traditions (Kymlicka 1995, cited by Martínez 2006). Applied in conjunction, autonomy relates more directly to the political and economic dimensions of self-determination, while self-government relates to the cultural and legal dimensions of the concept. Throughout the remainder of this Element, both concepts will be used according to this distinction (see Table 1).

2.4 Indigenous Self-Determination and the Extractive Industry

The ways in which Indigenous communities pursue self-determination are diverse and often contradictory. Previous ethnographic studies maintain that anti-extractivism is not, in fact, a defining characteristic of Indigenous peoples (Penfield 2019:88–89). These findings are consistent with other studies that have demonstrated that anti-extractivist goals only drive a small amount of Indigenous protest (Arce 2014; Arellano-Yanguas 2011).

Still other scholars defend a definition of self-determination as being equal to anti-extractivism (Cerqueira 2020; Lavinas Picqu 2014). Indigenous discourses on *Buen Vivir* ('the good life') disseminated in the 1990s by Indigenous intellectuals in the Andes have been particularly influential on anti-extractivist stances. Accordingly, living well entails utopian models of community life where humans and nonhumans coexist in equilibrium (see Territorio Indígena y Gobernanza [n. d.] for Indigenous definitions of *Buen Vivir*). Yet, even while various scholars still adhere to idealized versions of *Buen Vivir* (Gudynas 2014; Altmann 2013:291), others criticize these definitions for advancing essentialist views of Indigenous peoples. According to Stefanoni (2012), purist disseminators of *Buen Vivir* do not make the effort to articulate this philosophy, which allegedly emerges from the Indigenous cosmovision but does not always apply to the realities of everyday life in Indigenous communities. Over the centuries, European settlers and, more recently, extractive companies, mestizo communities, and criminal organizations have pushed Indigenous peoples into unproductive lands, resulting in them having to abandon their subsistence economies in search of low-skilled jobs (Partridge and Uquillas 1996).

In some context, extractive resources are the most easily available source of income for Indigenous communities to function both politically and economically. As such, the coexistence of Indigenous members and extractive companies is not always contentious (Penfield 2019). Negotiations with company employees for economic compensation, the hiring of Indigenous labor, and the provision of basic services by these companies also forms part of this coexistence. In this sense, Indigenous communities exchanging their lands for economic agreements may lead to improvement in some living conditions while negatively affecting others and, often, their environment.

Thus, the new constitutions of Bolivia and Ecuador include the principle of *Buen Vivir* but somehow make it compatible with the expansion of oil and mining industries in ecologically fragile ecosystems (Merino 2022; Gudynas 2014) Again, legal advocates tend to disagree with this position, arguing that the just implementation of Indigenous rights should not enable pacts that are destructive to Indigenous lands (Engle 2010:210). Extractive activities generally cause irreparable damage to environmental resources and local communities are forced to abandon their homes once company operations are completed. Following this logic, it is unlikely that sustainable living models can emerge from industrialized exploitation of nonrenewable natural resources (Stensrud 2019:160).

It is evident, therefore, that the way in which Indigenous peoples should exercise self-determination is a debated topic. The heterogeneity of Indigenous peoples across the American subcontinent and the different legal and economic contexts in which they operate mean that these groups remain divided over extractivism (Harder Horst 2020: ch. 13). Under such circumstances, a unified vision regarding how to exercise self-determination remains elusive. Looking beyond polarized positions in the literature regarding better understandings of self-determination, I examine Indigenous communities and their decisions regarding extractive projects together with the outcomes of these choices. In the following section, I develop the central argument of this Element.

2.4.1 The Argument

My comparative analysis shows two factors that impact self-determination outcomes in Indigenous communities: the use of favorable legal frameworks and the type of economic resources available. Together, these two factors allow Indigenous leaders to make demands and adopt decisions using Indigenous self-government structures, while enabling them to create or strengthen local economies and improve community life. The best illustration of this combination of using favorable legislation and accessing economic resources is the case of the community of Capulálpam de Méndez in Oaxaca, Mexico. The self-determination outcomes of this case are highly reflective of the discourses of international Indigenous organizations and environmental activists. Conversely, the community of Oxiacaque does not make use of such legal frameworks and mainly have access to resources derived from oil extraction. This case represents the worst-case scenario for Indigenous communities as community members face environmental degradation, health problems, political division, and cultural loss. The other cases lie somewhere in the middle with trade-offs between self-determination dimensions as defined in Section 1. I discuss these two factors further in Sections 2.1.1 and 2.1.2.

2.4.2 Favorable Legal Frameworks (FAF)

Since the 1990s, Latin American states have adopted a wide range of legislation in support of Indigenous rights. These laws generally recognize and validate Indigenous peoples' political, legal, and economic organization. According to Burguete (2013), for nascent Indigenous movements in the 1980s, the path to self-determination lay in "autonomy arrangements." Accordingly, ILO Convention 169 and the UNDRIP granted Indigenous peoples various rights, such as the right to organize their lives according to their own institutions, to customary law and culture over integrationist state policies, and also to prior consultation and compensation mechanisms regarding interventions on their land (Rodríguez-Garavito 2011).

Nonetheless, there is heterogeneity regarding how self-determination rights are legally implemented within and across countries. When Latin American nations gained independence from European powers, Indigenous peoples remained subject to internal colonialism, forced into subordinate interactions with national governments and new types of colonizers. These interactions became even more complex as new international actors, in the form of NGO employees, international officials, or extractive company employees arrived in Indigenous territories. Subsequently, Indigenous self-determination demands have taken different forms and are shaped by the local history of relations between Indigenous communities and outsiders.

For some Indigenous communities, where the municipal authority is the closest representative of oppressive regulations, gaining the right to participate in the election of these authorities has been a priority in the struggle toward self-determination (Burguete 2011). Other communities, facing criminalization by state justice systems, have directed most of their efforts to gaining the right to administer justice using customary law (Sieder 2012). With the global expansion of extractive interests, Indigenous demands for prior consultation against outside interests later became more salient.

In addition to the diversity of legal instruments created to address specific Indigenous demands within each country, Indigenous peoples' use of these laws also varies. Some communities have been able to ensure the enactment of favorable legislations and to use this for important aspects of their lives. Others lack the organizational capacity and mobilization resources to demand the enforcement of legislation, or are even unaware that they have specific rights. Often, Indigenous community members have been absorbed into the labor force by state or foreign companies, thus abandoning traditional economic activities such as agriculture, fishing, or hunting. While some of these communities have been able to restore the collective holding of lands and customary norms once companies have left, others have lost these and have been fully incorporated into municipal political organizations (Mattiace 2013).

This heterogeneity creates differences in how Indigenous communities embrace legislation, regardless of how progressive it may be. For instance, in Bolivia, the Morales government (2006–19) attempted to enhance Indigenous rights by creating Indigenous Originary Peasant Autonomies (AIOCs) which granted full political autonomy to Indigenous populations. However, the legal process of conversion to this system is full of political and administrative obstacles and few communities have the organizational resources to make the transition. Similarly, prior consultation has been widely used by politically organized Guarani communities (Falleti and Riofrancos 2018) but does not fulfill the same purposes for politically weak ethnic groups.

Self-determined vs. Integrationist Legal Practice

The specific use of existing legislation by Indigenous communities relates to what legal anthropologists define as legal practice. According to Brandon Hunter-Pazzara, in comparison with codified law, legal practice refers to the way laws are adopted and incorporated into everyday social and political life in particular communities. Legal practice may thus mirror codified laws but can also change or deviate over time (personal communication with Brandon Hunter-Pazzara, January 25, 2022). New institutionalism studies consistently show that local populations can assemble and reshape institutional arrangements to perform new functions (Cleaver and de Koning 2015).

Differences in Indigenous legal practices are evident in the cases analyzed in Section 3. Politically mobilized Indigenous groups typically expand the boundaries of pro-Indigenous legislation toward greater political autonomy (see Table 1). One such example is the community of Chetilla in Cajamarca (Peru) that abides by the *Rondas Campesinas* (Indigenous paroles) legal framework, which was initially recognized in the 1993 constitution and then supported with a specific law and regulation in 2003. The Chetilla community used Indigenous *Rondas* not only to resolve community conflicts, which is what the law provides for, but also as vehicles for anti-mining mobilization. Likewise, in Oaxaca, the community of Capulálpam de Méndez drew upon electoral autonomy and customary law to prohibit the entry of mining companies, even when this contravened federal law; similarly, the Guarani from Ingre (Bolivia) used the prior consultation legal framework to fight state attempts to reduce economic compensation derived from gas extraction. I classify these cases as self-determined legal practice (SLP) through which Indigenous leaders draw upon favorable legislation to enact substantive demands against the state.

In contrast, the communities of Oxiacaque and Homún (Mexico) are not able to make use of favorable legal frameworks. In these cases, substantive decisions concerning territorial affairs, political representation, and law enforcement remain the jurisdiction of municipal authorities or the federal government. For these communities, Indigenous rights remain rhetorical and state agencies retain control over decision-making (Burguete 2013). I classify these cases as integrationist legal practice (ILP). See Table 2 for an explanation of these categories.

2.4.3 Economic Resources for Indigenous Communities

The second factor guiding the argument in this Element, is the type of economic resource available to Indigenous communities. Multicultural policies in the

Table 2. Indigenous Uses of Favorable Legislation Frameworks

FAVORABLE LEGAL FRAMEWORKS (FLF)	EMPIRICAL EVIDENCE
Self-determined Legal Practice (SLP)	Indigenous groups use FLF to make substantive decisions over their territories and natural resources against decisions by the state
Integrationist Legal Practice (ILP)	Indigenous groups do not use FLF either because they are unaware of them, or because they choose not to apply these.

1990s were often referred to, in a variety of studies, as hollowed: they were not accompanied by resources that could make them a reality (Burguete 2013; Martinez Novo 2013; Hale 2002; Tapia 2000; Wade 1997). According to these studies, economic resources are indispensable for Indigenous peoples who are struggling for self-determination. Most Indigenous communities lack the means to implement economic projects that could improve their living conditions. Decades of poorly implemented state policies, along with the advancement of colonizers deeper into Indigenous territories, have resulted in high levels of Indigenous vulnerability. Most Indigenous environments are defined by the prevalence of difficult conditions, like hunger and disease, exacerbated by a lack of basic services such as water, energy, adequate inter-cultural education, health provision, and professional training.

For decades, international agencies such as the Fund for the Development of Indigenous Peoples of Latin America, several UN funds (among other agencies), and hundreds of NGOs have been the main providers of resources for Indigenous rights. Access to these funds, however, is highly competitive and they sometimes only benefit Indigenous leaders working at international and national levels. In addition, international agencies frequently work with state institutions to administer and allocate resources, the criteria for which are often decided in places divorced from Indigenous reality and thus risk being irrelevant for Indigenous communities.

Over the past twenty years, the growth in social conflict resulting from increasing operations of extractive industries has led extractive companies to strengthen local development programs through corporate social responsibility (CSR) frameworks in the hope of gaining community support (Yakovleva y Vazquez- Brust 2012). With local development as a slogan, CSR attempts to provide neighboring populations (mostly Indigenous) with education, health, and cultural services (O'Faircheallaigh and Ali 2008; Dashwood 2007; Haslam 2004). Nonetheless, several studies highlight that these programs increase local discontent (Conde and LeBillon 2017; Himley 2014). As company employees retain control of economic resources and program design, the programs are frequently not culturally appropriate, companies fail to fulfill the agreements made with community members, and/or environmental impacts are greater than anticipated (Guarneros-Meza and Madrigal 2022; Gil 2009). Community division tends to follow CSR, and many consider that companies use social programs to coopt and demobilize community members. Equally discouraging, most of these programs disappear once companies leave the extraction sites.

In parallel with corporate initiatives, Latin American governments have passed decentralization policies aimed at expanding states' distributive capacity (Haslam and Heidrich 2016). Mining and hydrocarbon royalties, trusts, and development funds, among others, were created in countries such as Peru, Ecuador, Colombia, and Bolivia to distribute extractive revenues to under-resourced rural municipalities. This was done to create economic wealth in resource-rich regions frequently inhabited by extremely poor communities (Viale and Cruzado 2012; Arellano-Yanguas 2011). In a similar spirit, a mining fund (*Fondo Minero*) was created in Mexico to reinvest the taxes paid by mining companies in development programs for mineral-producing municipalities (Guarneros-Meza 2019).

However, weak administrative capacity by subnational governments hinders efficient investment to sustain development after extractive companies leave (Conde and LeBillon 2017; Arellano-Yanguas 2011). In most cases, resource distribution tends to follow integrationist models by expanding social programs in the poorest communities. Social programs, however, although important for ensuring the survival of vulnerable groups, are generally blind to the specific needs and expectations of Indigenous communities (López Bárcenas 2013; Blaser et al. 2004). Worse still, they contribute to reinforcing stereotypes regarding Indigenous peoples, as well as discrimination and exclusion (Stavenhagen 1992).

Overall, both corporate and state distributive regimes fail to provide local populations with viable economic, social, or environmental alternatives in the long term (Olvera 2020). For the most part, extractive companies and state authorities retain decision-making abilities regarding how funds are allocated. Indigenous communities are rarely allowed to design and implement projects using these resources. As a result, new conflicts have generally followed the implementation of distributive instruments (Bebbington and Bury 2009).

Even when Indigenous organizations face significant restrictions on accessing private or public funding, increased state budgets (derived from the extractive industry or the rise in national and international funding for the conservation of Indigenous biodiverse territories) do create some opportunities for

Indigenous direct management of economic resources. I develop this further in the next subsection.

Nonextractive Resources (NER)

I consider nonextractive resources (NER) as all types of funding not based on the implementation of extractive operations and aimed at strengthening Indigenous rights. These resources generally come from international agencies or national public offices responsible for Indigenous affairs, environmental protection, or nonextractive industries. Examples of NER are funds to boost Indigenous economies through sustainable agriculture, cattle raising, fishing, forestry harvesting, and tourism, among others.[4]

From the cases, we learned that the allocation of NER is independent of Indigenous use of favorable legal frameworks (FLF). Nonetheless, there is no systematic information regarding Indigenous access to these funds. The amount of NER that governments or international actors actually allocate for Indigenous communities, how these resources are spent, and the results for Indigenous communities have not been systematically documented. For this research, I have relied upon secondary sources to identify cases of Indigenous negotiation for NER. In addition, I interviewed state officials working with Indigenous communities and examined the database of Indigenous peoples created by the Ministry of Culture of Peru and the Observatory of Participation, Conflict, and the Environment created by FLACSO (Latin American Faculty of Social Sciences), Mexico and De Montfort University, UK.

In Section 3, I examine two cases of NER in Mexico. The first is the Indigenous municipality of Capulálpam de Méndez (Oaxaca), where community members employ a SLP and have been able to build sustainable economic models and reject mining. The second is in Homún (Yucatán) where, despite the community's ILP, some Indigenous members have been able to access funding and implement ecotourism for the benefit of most members. However, unlike Capulálpam, Homún is still struggling to prevent the development of a mega pig farm that would threaten their lands. In both cases, Indigenous economies have improved but with different consequences for the community's self-determination outcomes.

Extractive Resources (ER)

I consider extractive resources (ER) as all types of funding directly derived from the operation of extractive projects. As with NER, there is no official information

---

[4] In Peru, environmental agencies promote community reserves in partnership with Indigenous communities and SLP Indigenous organizations fund international resources for development and the protection of biodiversity.

regarding the amount and further use of ER by Indigenous communities. For Bolivia, I drew upon secondary sources documenting prior consultation negotiations, the legislation on prior consultation compensations, and interviews with Indigenous leaders. For Peru, I relied upon secondary sources including the information on Indigenous peoples available on the Ministry of Culture website. In Mexico, I accessed secondary sources documenting Indigenous negotiations with extractive companies. I also built upon the information on socio-environmental conflicts available from the Observatory of Participation, Conflict, and the Environment created by FLACSO and De Montfort University.

Indigenous access to ER is also independent of the operation of SLP or ILP. However, the cases examined in Section 3 shed light on the prevalence of informal negotiations between Indigenous individuals and company employees in the case of ILP. Generally, the motivation for these negotiations is to obtain leaders' compliance with extraction by compensating for damages to the local environment or any other damage resulting from extractive operations. This is the case in Oxiacaque (Tabasco) where lack of transparency is evidenced as one of the main problems for this type of negotiation. Informal economic agreements, frequently reached behind closed doors, raise suspicion among community members regarding the commitments made by their representatives.

Conversely, in the community of Ingre (Chuquisaca, Bolivia) governed by SLP, access to these resources takes place through formal negotiations between community representatives and extractive companies. Indigenous members decide how much to ask from extractive companies, and they decide how to use the resources for community projects in community assemblies. After a consensus is reached, leaders negotiate with the companies. Table 3 summarizes the types of economic resources available to Indigenous communities.

Finally, I also examined cases of no resources (NR) where neither NER nor ER are available. These are the cases of Chetilla and Atahualpa in Peru where Indigenous communities depend almost entirely on subsistence activities which they sometimes supplement with social programs and state services derived from small municipal budgets or based on political will.

2.5 Preliminary Hypotheses

My comparative case analysis gave rise to the formulation of some preliminary hypotheses which may be tested by other scholars interested in this topic. Indigenous legal practices (SLP or ILP), together with the type of economic resources (ER or NER) or the absence of resources (NR) available for Indigenous communities, shape self-determination outcomes in rural municipalities. Different combinations of the two factors have different outcomes. In

Table 3. Economic Resources Available for Indigenous Communities

TYPE	DEFINITION	INSTRUMENTS OF FUNDING
Extractive Resources (ER)	Economic resources provided by the state or extractive companies conditioned on Indigenous approval of resource extraction.	Compensations, rents, salaries, micro-credits.
Non-extractive Resources (NER)	Economic resources derived from international or public funding aimed at creating sustainable economies within Indigenous territories	State development programs for agriculture, state development programs for rural tourism, ecological conservation programs, technical support.
No Resources (NR)	There are not resources available for Indigenous communities	Indigenous subsistence activities, social programs, services derived from the will of politicians.

most cases, I find that Indigenous community leaders make important trade-offs in order to obtain partial gains. I advance the following hypotheses based on my findings.

In Capulálpam de Méndez, SLP and access to NER enabled a full exercise of self-determination in its political, economic, cultural, and legal dimensions. Thus:

H1 Indigenous communities exercising a self-determined legal practice and receiving economic resources from a nonextractive actor are more likely to prohibit unwanted projects and strengthen local economies for the benefit of community members. In the process of guiding their economic development these communities enhance their cultures and enforce their customary norms.

In Ingre, SLP and access to ER enabled a partial exercise of self-determination in its economic and cultural dimensions, but the political and legal dimensions are reduced. Thus:

H2 Indigenous communities exercising a self-determined legal practice and accepting resources from extractive actors are likely to implement economic projects for the benefit of community members. These communities use their cultural identities to negotiate with extractive actors, which creates incentives for cultural preservation. However, their ability to prohibit the expansion of extractive projects in their lands is reduced. Because these communities must share their territory with extractive employees and infrastructure, their ability to enforce customary norms inside their territories is also limited.

In Chetilla and Atahualpa, Indigenous communities have SLP but NR. They can exercise partial self-determination as its political, cultural, and legal dimensions are met, while economic self-determination remains unfulfilled. Thus:

H3 Indigenous communities exercising a self-determined legal practice but with no economic resources to create economic alternatives for their members can successfully reject extractive companies, keep their cultures alive and customary norms enforced, but still depend on the state to supplement their living.

In Homún, Indigenous use of ILP and access to NER resulted in a partial exercise of self-determination with an increase in the economic, political, cultural, and legal dimensions, although still with limited results. Thus:

H4 Indigenous communities abiding by integrationist legal frameworks and with access to economic resources from nonextractive actors can improve local economies, increase their ability to reject unwanted projects and also revive their cultures and develop legal mechanisms for self-government, but not sufficiently for full self-determination.

In Oxiacaque, Indigenous communities with ILP and access to ER do not exercise self-determination as none of the dimensions of this right are present. Thus:

H5 Indigenous communities abiding by integrationist legal frameworks and with access to economic resources derived from extractive actors face important challenges to self-govern their territories according to their customary laws. They suffer economic scarcities, cultural loss, environmental degradation, and are incapable of rejecting the state and extractive companies.

Table 4 summarizes the self-determination outcomes derived from the hypotheses presented above.

2.6 Methodology

The theory presented in this study stems from the analysis of six cases of Indigenous communities living in rural municipalities in Bolivia, Peru, and Mexico. In all six cases most members self-identify with an Indigenous ethnic group, the communities are legally recognized as Indigenous, and they form part of or comprise an entire municipal jurisdiction. I use a comparative case

Table 4. Preliminary Hyphoteses

ECONOMIC RESOURCES	FAVORABLE LEGAL FRAMEWORK	
	SLP	**ILP**
NER	H1 Indigenous communities have political, economic, legal and cultural self-determination	H4 Indigenous communities *increase* political, economic, legal and cultural self-determination, but full-self-determination has yet to be achieved
ER	H2 Indigenous communities have economic and cultural self-determination but there is a loss of political and legal self-determination	H5 Indigenous communities do not have any form of self-determination
NR	H3 Indigenous communities have political, cultural and legal self-determination but they lack economic self-determination	*No empirical instances were examined*

methodology to achieve an in-depth understanding of cases, and the identification of patterns and differences across cases. The study rests upon a comparison of Indigenous communities with contrasting experiences of extractive projects and different self-determination outcomes. The cases examined are: Capulálpam de Méndez (Mexico), Ingre (Bolivia), Chetilla (Peru), Homún (Mexico), Oxiacaque (Mexico), and Atahualpa (Peru).

2.6.1 Case Selection and Time Frame

The lens used to analyze Indigenous self-determination is that of extractive conflicts. In much of the specialized literature on Latin America's Indigenous peoples, the extractive industry represents a major challenge to the realization of self-determination. Extractive projects jeopardize the right of Indigenous peoples to reject unwanted projects (autonomy) and threaten existing forms of territorial management as well as Indigenous institutions, economies, and cultural traditions (self-government). The salience of extractive conflicts in

Latin America has led scholars and activists to develop national and international databases to systematize information regarding the identity and location of communities in conflict, the identity of extractive companies and their countries of origin, and the causes, development, and outcomes of conflict, among other information.

Intuitively, it could be assumed that national government ideology and how national constitutions address Indigenous rights impact self-determination outcomes in Indigenous communities. However, much evidence exists suggesting that these two factors have no impact on the advancement of extractive projects in Indigenous lands (Merino 2022; Torres-Wong 2019; Poweska 2017; Gudynas 2012). On the contrary, I emphasize Indigenous use of legal frameworks and the economic resources available to Indigenous communities.

To obtain variation in national ideology and constitutional settings, I selected Indigenous municipalities from three countries: Bolivia, Mexico, and Peru. Since the beginning of the commodity boom (2000), these three countries have been ruled by both right- and left-wing governments. In addition, Bolivia has some of the most progressive policies regarding self-determination as these are included in the constitution and have been legally implemented. In the case of Mexico, it recognized self-determination in the constitution as a result of the Zapatista uprising in 1994 and the San Andres Accords signed between the government and the Indigenous movement. However, it has yet to fully implement the policy outlined in the Accords and only some states have some form of implementation legislation. Peru does not recognize self-determination in its constitution.

For the case selection, I drew upon the Observatory for Mining Conflicts in Latin America (OCMAL), the Global Atlas of Environmental Justice (EJAtlas) developed by the Institute of Environmental Science and Technology at the Autonomous University of Barcelona (Temper et al. 2015), and the Observatory of Participation, Conflict, and the Environment in Mexico developed by FLACSO and De Montfort University.

In the three countries, FLF are evident, as well as cases of SLP and ILP. This allowed me to select Indigenous municipalities ruled by different Indigenous legal practices. Extractive resources are prominent in Bolivia, Mexico, and Peru. In addition, I found cases of NER in Mexico and of NR in Peru. This variation allowed for the selection of Indigenous municipalities with access to ER, NER, and NR.

The period under analysis covers the decade of the 1990s, when multicultural policies began to be converted into legal frameworks, and continues until January 2022 when the research concluded. Over these thirty years, I examine the creation of FLF, the availability and distribution of economic resources to Indigenous communities, how Indigenous leaders adopted political and economic decisions regarding these resources, the emergence of conflict and/or negotiation between community members and extractive companies, and how communities' use of ER, NER or NR impacts the life of Indigenous members and their collective goals.

2.6.2 Data Collection

The cases examined in this study draw on data collected during fieldwork undertaken between 2011 and 2022. The research included eighty-five semi-structured interviews with Indigenous leaders, extractive company employees, state officials, and local scholars in Bolivia, Peru, and Mexico. I undertook several visits to the municipalities of Capulálpam de Méndez, Chetilla, Homún, Oxiacaque, and Atahualpa during this time and was able to participate in different events in which Indigenous communities demanded self-determination vis-à-vis the state and extractive companies (community assemblies, local forums, marches, protests, legal mobilization events). I was unable to visit Ingre in Chuquisaca, Bolivia and relied on interviews with Indigenous leaders, scholars, and NGO employees who had worked with Guarani communities for several decades. In 2015, I conducted several visits to the El Chaco region, home to the Guarani, and was able to rely upon the contacts made during those visits to secure phone interviews for this research. To supplement information regarding Guarani negotiations on ER, I relied on the database of prior consultations in Bolivia created by Falleti and Riofrancos (2018) and updated by Zaremberg and Torres-Wong (2018).

Additional secondary sources included scholarly studies, municipal development reports in each country, and newspaper articles related to the emergence of conflict, Indigenous self-determination demands, and negotiations on different types of economic resources (ER and NER).

2.6.3 Scholarly Work on Self-Determination

Much of the existing literature on Indigenous self-determination is legal and focuses on how national and international courts define this right and resolve legal controversies around it (Graham 2004; Anaya 2000; Daes 2000; Scheinin 2000). I argue that self-determination encompasses more than decisions over specific legal complaints or idealized legal definitions of Indigenous rights. There is a great disconnect between Indigenous political organizations operating at the international level with ties to legal activists and access to international forums and underresourced Indigenous leaders struggling to achieve self-determination at the community level. Rather than being based on romanticized court decisions with little impact on local Indigenous societies, self-determination is a process developed within Indigenous territories on a daily basis through negotiations and conflict with extractive companies, state actors, and criminal organizations, among others. In this regard, I emphasize that legal frameworks addressing self-determination matter to the extent that they are used by Indigenous communities to materialize their political goals.

Another school of thought rests upon definitions of self-determination that are based narrowly on anti-extractivism (Picq 2014). According to these, the active promotion of extractive industries by the state is the main obstacle to the realization of the right to self-determination (Poweska 2017). Similarly, various studies on prior consultation in countries such as Bolivia, Peru, Ecuador, Colombia, and Mexico define the failures of Indigenous participation as based on Indigenous groups' inability to veto consulted projects (Torres-Wong 2019; Leifsen et al. 2018; Flemmer and Schilling-Vacaflor, 2016). Such studies offer only a partial picture of the right to self-determination, as it encompasses economic, political, and cultural dimensions that extend beyond the approval of projects (Gouritin and Aguilar 2017). Using prior consultation to examine self-determination can be reductionist, as it hinders the examination of broader political processes that take place inside communities. Other scholars study self-determination through the struggles of some Indigenous organizations that gather various Indigenous communities for the creation of Indigenous autonomous governments (Merino 2020; Sieder and Barrera 2017). These studies, however valuable, do not represent the reality of most Indigenous communities struggling to gain political and economic power within the structures of rural municipal jurisdictions.

In this Element, I advocate for territorialized and more dynamic definitions of self-determination. I frame self-determination as a complex process existing on a continuum. In this process, Indigenous leaders often make trade-offs to achieve minimum levels of well-being. Extractivist projects represent a constant threat to the natural environments of Indigenous peoples; however, under specific conditions, my cases show that they can represent an opportunity to secure economic autonomy. Section 3 examines the contrasting results obtained by Indigenous communities and it attempts to illustrate their heterogeneity by emphasizing their different legal abilities and economic resources. The cases confirm that Indigenous struggles are mostly guided by the desire to improve living conditions, but without undergoing assimilation (Engel 2010). The paths taken toward this goal, however, lead to different outcomes.

3 The Cases

3.1 Indigenous Self-Determination and Extractive Industries

This section compares the self-determination outcomes of six Indigenous communities living in rural municipalities in Bolivia, Peru, and Mexico. In some of these communities, Indigenous leaders embrace anti-extractivist goals, while in others self-determination is pursued through extractive revenues. Emphasis is placed on Indigenous ability to use existing legal frameworks and available economic resources to improve life in Indigenous communities. I examine the cases of Capulálpam de Méndez (Mexico), Chetilla (Peru), Ingre (Bolivia), Homún (Mexico), Oxiacaque (Mexico), and Atahualpa (Peru). Differences in the use of favorable legal frameworks (SLP or ILP) and in types of economic resources available for community projects (ER, NER. or NR) shape the self-determination outcomes.

3.1.1 The Zapoteca People from Capulálpam de Méndez in Oaxaca, Mexico

Oaxaca is a state in Southern Mexico widely recognized as home to the most sizable Indigenous population in the country, with 65.7 percent of residents identifying with one of the eighteen ethnic groups in the state. In 1990, the Constitution of Oaxaca incorporated the right of Indigenous municipalities to elect their own authorities using customary norms. This became official in 1995 within a context of widespread political contention that originated in the Zapatista insurrection, with Indigenous communities in Oaxaca demonstrating on the streets to demand autonomy and self-government (Educa 2020). The new system, known as *Usos y Costumbres* ("Customs and Traditions"), prioritized Indigenous electoral practices over the traditional party system and today it prevails in 418 of the 517 municipalities in the state.

While Oaxaca made important legal progress regarding Indigenous rights, multicultural laws still subordinate Indigenous normative systems to national laws (Educa 2020; Martínez 2006). However, over the years, SLP by most organized and politically skilled communities has pushed the boundaries of *Usos y Costumbres* toward greater political autonomy. In 2005, a conflict with the Canadian mining company Continuum Resources broke out in the Zapoteca municipality of Capulálpam de Méndez, located in the northern mountains known as Sierra de Juarez.[5] The population opposed mining activities on the basis of their environmental impact. Mobilizing the support of nearby communities, Indigenous municipal authorities initiated a socio-legal battle against the company, which finally withdrew the project in 2011. In 2020, anti-mining leaders informed the media that, after five years of litigation, the Third District Court had recognized Capulálpam de Méndez as the legitimate owner of their ancestral land (Perez Alfonso 2020).[6]

---

[5] The Zapoteca are the largest ethnic group in Oaxaca followed by the Mixteca and the Mazatecos.

[6] In Oaxaca, 44 percent of the territory has been granted to mining and it has one of the highest levels of violence connected with mining projects (Observatory of Participation, Conflict and the Environment n.d.).

Several times Capulálpams have demonstrated their capacity to take action against the state in defense of their natural resources. In the 1980s, Capulálpam de Méndez, together with neighboring communities, initiated a long process to recover custodianship of their forests from private companies. With a population of 1,597 this community is notable for having consolidated a system of self-government based on Indigenous customary norms and cultural values.[7] Like most municipalities in Oaxaca, Capulálpam is governed by the *Usos y Costumbres* system and elects municipal authorities through customary law. In parallel, it is recognized as an agrarian community in terms of Mexico's agrarian law, holding collective property of lands, and as an Indigenous community according to the law of Oaxaca. The agrarian authority is the *Comisariado de Bienes Comunales* (Commissariat of Community Goods), responsible for administering community lands and natural resources. There is also a *Consejo de Caracterizados* (Elders Council) which represents Indigenous authority and provides advice to municipal and agrarian authorities, functioning as a legislative body inside Capulálpam's municipal jurisdiction (Capulálpam de Méndez 2018; Chávez and Valtierra-Pacheco 2018).

The General Community Assembly is the most important mechanism for collective decision-making above the Elders Council. This assembly is the deliberative institution par excellence in rural Oaxaca and is considered the ultimate expression of Indigenous self-government (Torres-Mazuera and Recondo 2022). For Capulálpams, the General Community Assembly is the central piece of their customary norms system and prevails over municipal and agrarian authorities.

Historically, Capulálpam was a mining town. Mineral extraction had existed in the region since 1775 and was the main source of employment for male community members. Respondents noted that people were able to send their children to schools in the city of Oaxaca because of their work in the mine. However, there is also a generalized perception of mining companies' exploitation of Indigenous labor (Mendez 2017). When extractive activities came to a halt in the 1990s, people were forced to migrate to other cities in search of jobs. Nevertheless, a strong sense of community and shared cultural values preserved unity among community members (Capulálpam de Méndez 2018). The *cargo* system, an emblematic Indigenous tradition through which individuals progress politically by providing different types of free services (or *tequio*) to the community is a pillar of Capulálpam's political organization.

---

[7] The population size is an estimate from 2017 official records; when temporary residents are included, the population totals 4,000.

Strengthening Indigenous Economy through NER

The lack of economic opportunities prompted many Capulálpams to migrate to Oaxaca, where they found jobs in government. From these positions, Indigenous professionals have sought ways to improve living conditions in their hometown. Such is the case of Ricardo Ramirez, a community member of Capulálpam and an agronomist who served as a state program manager in CONAFOR (the National Forestry Commission or *Comisión Nacional Forestal*) promoting sustainable management of the forest. He has directed efforts and resources to foster this development model in Capulálpam and neighboring communities from the Sierra de Juárez: "Economic resources are not sufficient to orient community behavior, each community has their conditions ... Private exploitation of the forest left negative perceptions in the communities because they had little room to participate" (CONAFOR 2007:19).

Various state agencies, such as the National Commission for the Development of Indigenous Populations (*Comisión Nacional para el Desarrollo de los Pueblos Indígenas* or CDI) and the Ministry of Tourism (*Secretaría de Turismo*) followed CONAFOR in promoting a sustainable economy in Capulálpam. These agencies provided Indigenous leaders with technical and economic support to develop ecotourism. Assisted by the Ministry of Tourism, Capulálpam applied to the *Pueblos Mágicos* ("Magic Towns") federal program aimed at expanding tourism in Mexico's rural municipalities. As part of this program, Capulálpam has been able to access federal resources to promote tourism since 2008.

Through the General Community Assembly, community members approved the use of state resources to develop their economy and they provided the wood and nonremunerated community labor or *tequio* to build the project infrastructure. Today, the community welcomes tourists from Mexico and abroad. However, community leaders warn residents to keep foreigners under supervision, in order to avoid "contamination of the community livelihood" (Torres-Wong 2019).

Over the last decade, Capulálpam has become a model for Indigenous economic development based on ecotourism and the sustainable use of forestry resources. Activities such as carbon capturing, sale of forestry belts, and hydraulic services form part of Capulálpam's economy. Four community-owned companies are responsible for creating employment for young people. There are also several companies created by different community groups selling wooden furniture and toys and providing alternative medical services based on the Indigenous tradition (Capulálpam de Méndez 2018).

In comparison with adjacent Indigenous municipalities, Capulálpam de Méndez represents quality of community life. Most of the population have their basic needs met and have access to functioning education and health care (Bartra 2013; Bray and Merino 2004:153). Furthermore, the majority of residents do not live on subsistence activities; nor do they need to migrate to other cities in search of employment (Municipal Council for Sustainable Rural Development 2009:164).

SLP against the Mining Industry

In 2004, the Canadian mining company Continuum Resources began exploration and exploitation activities for silver and gold on land that formed part of Capulálpam de Méndez (Mendez 2017:30). Studies carried out by the company had shown that sizable amounts of these valuable minerals still existed in the area, and could be extracted using the open-pit technique. At first, Continuum Resources operated in locations outside the municipality. However, the company gradually started exploring areas near spring water sources. This concerned the municipal authorities, and caused tension between the population and mining employees (Aquino 2011).

In 2005, the General Community Assembly decided to prohibit mining and demanded that the government cancel all mining concessions in its territory. Against constitutional norms granting the federal government authority over the national subsoil, Capulálpams claimed their right to govern their territories according to their own normative and political systems. Opposition to mining was led by the three local authorities: the agrarian, the Indigenous, and the municipal. Various street protests, road blockages, and acts of disobedience (vandalizing the mine's premises and equipment) took place (Guarneros-Meza and Torres-Wong 2022), with neighboring organizations joining the anti-mining struggle and supporting Capulálpam by providing mobilization resources and spreading anti-mining sentiment.

Representatives from Continuum Resources went to Capulálpam to offer jobs and development opportunities to the young people; however, the authorities remained firm in their decision to reject the mining project (Personal communication with the Commissariat of Community Goods, October 2018). Capulálpam's anti-mining stance was also supported by state officials associated with the forestry administration, such as the Agrarian Attorney (or *Procurador Agrario*) in Oaxaca, one of the most important state authorities regarding land affairs. When asked about his understanding of the conflict, the Agrarian Attorney conceded that: "Capulálpam has the right to decide about its territory because it is an Agrarian Community, and the mine is on community lands" (Torres-Wong and Jimenez-Sandoval 2022:6).

In addition to opposing the mining company, Capulálpam was faced with a neighboring municipality that supported the mining project. Natividad, located next to Capulálpam, was created after the discovery of a gold and silver mine in 1775 from which it acquired its name, *Mina de la Natividad* (Mine of the Nativity). At its peak, the mine attracted workers from all over the country, including members of Capulálpam. However, unlike Capulálpam, Natividad is not an Indigenous community and economic alternatives did not develop after the mining companies left. As a result, Natividad approved the reactivation of the mine. These differences resulted in conflict between residents of the two municipalities and Natividad became a pro-mining traitor in the eyes of the Capulálpam authorities (Torres-Wong and Jimenez-Sandoval 2022).

A legal battle began in an attempt to resolve the dispute over which of the two municipalities had the right to decide whether mining activities were to move forward. Before the conflict, Natividad residents had had free access to Capulálpam lands, and water was supplied by Capulálpam at no cost. However, as tensions increased, Capulálpam prohibited access to wood and cut the water supply to Natividad. Anti-mining leaders sought to force Natividad to desist from its legal claim. Faced with water scarcity, the leaders of Natividad acquiesced. However, despite regaining their access to water, they are now required to pay an annual fee. Natividad has sought alternative solutions to the conflict, yet its petitions have been ignored, and Capulálpam has refused to attend the conciliation assemblies organized to resolve the conflict (Torres-Wong and Jimenez-Sandoval 2022).

In the end, Capulálpam prevailed, and Natividad is now considered part of Capulálpam territory but with no power to approve projects. Respondents in Natividad complained about the attitude of Capulálpam's leaders: "It's not a magic town, I call it a tragic town … they have so much but want more" (personal communication with a resident of Natividad, October 2018). Anti-mining leaders refuse to accept Natividad's petition to accept mining, but they have not shared the benefits of their flourishing economy with their neighbors.

Self-Determination as Anti-Extractivism

Capulálpams have achieved outstanding levels of self-determination in its political, legal, economic, and cultural dimensions. Likewise, the case of Capulálpam de Méndez is closest to the ideal of Indigenous self-determination as envisioned by environmentalists and international discourses on *Buen Vivir*. Self-determined use of the *Usos y Costumbres* legislation that granted them municipal autonomy enabled Capulálpams to confront pro-mining state regulations. According to Indigenous leaders, customary norms prevail over state laws and are enforced by the General Community Assembly, portrayed as the head of the municipality (CONAFOR 2007). Self-determined legal practice, together with NER, enabled Indigenous leaders to undertake partnerships with state agencies while maintaining control of their economy. Through NER, Indigenous leaders were able to strengthen their government by increasing their ability to implement economic projects that benefit the community. Cultural practices such as the *tequio* and the *cargo* system, considered the glue that holds community members together, permeated the entire process.

The infrastructure that was built for ecotourism and related services contributed to economic growth within Capulálpam's territory, creating new economic ventures that have proven attractive to the young people of the community. The autonomy of Capulálpam was not compromised by NER, regarding whether or not to work with the mining industry. On the contrary, it created conditions for an economic model that undermined the value of mining and the productive infrastructure that accompanies it (Guarneros-Meza and Torres-Wong 2022). Community members are no longer forced to migrate in search of economic alternatives. Furthermore, Indigenous leaders have aligned Capulálpam's cultural values with sustainable development. Capulálpams now publicize eco-friendly services, linking their cultural identity to the defense of the environment.

Indigenous authorities emphasize that it is the community that decides what is done in Capulálpam, and all the authorities must obey. The combination of SLP with NER created a virtuous circle, in which community members were incentivized to preserve their territory and reinforce cultural practices. The case also demonstrates that even within the same territory, communities do not all have the same opportunities, as in the case of Natividad which has been incapable of overcoming mining dependence.

3.1.2 The Guarani People from Ingre in Chuquisaca, Bolivia

The Guarani People are the third largest Indigenous ethnic group in Bolivia, after the Quechua and the Aymara, and are spread across the departments of Santa Cruz, Tarija, and Chuquisaca, within the El Chaco region. Together with thirty-three smaller ethnic groups mostly inhabiting the Amazon basin, the Guarani comprise the Indigenous peoples from the lowlands. In 1990, lowlands Indigenous communities undertook "the first march for the defense of territory and dignity" covering the 640 kilometers from the Amazon to La Paz City, demanding that the Bolivian government respect Indigenous cultures. In 1995, the Bolivian constitution recognized the multicultural and plurinational nature of the country (Cooke 2013), and in 1996 the government passed the INRA law (National Institute of Agrarian Reform) with the objective of recognizing, among other things, the collective property rights of Indigenous communities.

Multicultural recognition created conditions for the multiplication of Indigenous demands centered on Indigenous cultural distinction. For the Guarani from El Chaco, where most Bolivian gas reserves are located, their fight focused on gaining political power over the oil companies. In 2005, in a context of widespread Indigenous mobilization against neoliberal policies, a new hydrocarbon law (Hydrocarbon Law 3058) was passed, affording Indigenous communities the right to prior consultation and including the power to veto unwanted projects (Hydrocarbon Law 3058, Article 115). In addition, the law granted Indigenous communities the right to obtain economic compensation for all social and environmental damages resulting from oil-related operations (Hydrocarbon Law 3058, Article 17).

When Evo Morales came to power in 2006 a new political constitution was approved, and prior consultation became a constitutional right. Indigenous peoples were legally recognized as socio-environmental monitors of hydrocarbon operations with the right to receive salaries from oil companies. This right was made effective in Supreme Decree 29103 in 2007 and was recognized in the new constitution of 2009. Since 2009, Indigenous peoples have also been granted the choice to become Indigenous Originary Peasant Autonomies (AIOCs) with full political independence from municipal authorities.[8]

The Guarani communities are among those ethnic groups that have most benefited from favorable legislation. Extraction of hydrocarbons had occurred in El Chaco long before Guarani communities began to reoccupy their lands. Up until approximately three decades ago, Guarani members had lived in semi-slavery conditions, working for powerful rancher elites for nearly a century (*Sistema de haciendas- hacienda* system). Guarani's organizing structures and political goals were thus shaped by their ongoing experiences of conflict and negotiation with hydrocarbon companies (Humphreys-Bebbington 2012:138). Over the years and aided by NGOs and the Catholic Church, Guarani leaders have been able to build strong political organization.[9]

Together with other Indigenous ethnic groups from the lowlands, Guarani communities formed an Indigenous organization, *Comunidades Indígenas del Oriente Boliviano* (Indigenous Communities from Eastern Bolivia or CIDOB), in 1982. Five years later, the Guarani created the *Asamblea General del Pueblo Guarani* (General Assembly of the Guarani People or APG). Over the years, the

---

[8] Conversion into AIOCs is a complex process fraught with political and economic obstacles; only a few Indigenous groups have completed conversion (Lopez Flores and Makaran 2020), and among them are the Guarani People from Charagua Iyambe. Territorial fragmentation and internal division prevent the AIOCs from being an attractive model for most Indigenous groups (Lopez Flores and Makaran 2020). Moreover, some leaders argue that AIOCs weaken the Asamblea del Pueblo Guarani's (Assembly of the Guarani People, or APG) decision-making capacity. Extractive resources, negotiated through prior consultations, continue to be the most available source of financing for local development.

[9] These institutions bought lands from the government for Guarani members to resettle in communities after they had escaped the estates.

APG acquired notable convening and coordination powers (Caurey 2015). Today, Guarani communities are organized into twenty-nine captaincies, politically subordinate to the APG, with the General Community Assembly as the most important deliberative and decision-making mechanism (Guarani Autonomous Government Charagua Iyambae n.d.). In addition, every level in the organization (community, regional, and national), has its own assembly which makes decisions over territorial organization and economic development (Torres-Wong 2019).

Well-established mechanisms of deliberation and decision-making have enabled Guarani groups to hold the government accountable for their rights. Regardless of how progressive the legal frameworks in Bolivia are, the country's dependence on gas revenues prevents these laws from fulfilling the functions that many Indigenous rights supporters envisioned, and thus alternative development models, headed by Indigenous peoples, have not proliferated as many expected. The Guarani are among those who more readily complied with gas extraction and currently use the rights obtained to negotiate ER.

The Captaincy of Ingre and Gas Revenues

The Captaincy of Ingre is one of nine Guarani Captaincies (*capitanías*) operating in the department of Chuquisaca. Ingre comprises 10 small communities with a population totaling 1,000. All nine Indigenous captaincies are accountable to the Council of Guarani Captains of Chuquisaca (*Consejo de Capitanes Guaraníes de Chuquisaca* or CCCH). Ingre did not convert to the AIOC system and continues to form part of the rural municipality of San Pablo Huacareta in the province of Hernado Siles, governed by the political party system. With the commodity boom and the peak in the price of hydrocarbons, extractive revenues have become increasingly important for Chuquisaca and the seventy-six communities inhabiting this department.

Traditional Guarani economies are based on agriculture, semi-subsistence–based farming, hunting, fishing, and the gathering of wild plants and fruits (Manos Unidas n.d.). Migration rates among Guarani communities have typically been high (Cauthin 2017; Healy 1987). Even after gaining freedom from the estates, Indigenous members still migrated temporarily to the nearest cities or sought employment with their former *patrones* to obtain an income. When extractive operations in Chuquisaca began, Guarani communities in Ingre were able to use prior consultation to ensure that oil companies paid compensations for using their land.[10]

---

[10] There are no official records on prior consultations in Bolivia. As of 2018, academic studies identified only twelve consultations in the department of Chuquisaca (Falleti and Riofrancos 2018; Zaremberg and Torres-Wong 2018).

In 2012, Ingre was consulted about seismic processing for gas exploration by the state oil company YPFB. The current Guarani Captain of Ingre explained in an interview that a fixed percentage is legally stipulated regarding the amount of economic compensation per type of hydrocarbon operation. Indigenous communities know what to ask for and use this knowledge to demand that companies disburse the funds before projects begin. Leaders are also able to negotiate the building of infrastructure or the provision of services once extractive operations start. All communities impacted by hydrocarbon projects participate in the consultation. Community members use *Asambleas Zonales* (regional assemblies), to decide how to spend the funds. The resources may be invested in a project shared by various communities or each community may receive funds to develop their own small projects (personal communication with Guarani Captain of Ingre, January 14, 2021).

Leaders in Ingre consider that gas revenues have brought economic improvements for Indigenous peoples. Community members are now able to find employment in oil companies as part of the labor force, provide catering services, or work in social and environmental affairs. With the compensation money, leaders have created community companies to promote agrobiodiverse products grown exclusively in Guarani ecosystems. In the words of the current Captain of Ingre:

> Now we have the capacity to go to the cities and build our offices there, we have a food processing plant owned by the Guarani nation, we are moving forward, . . . we are trying to obtain the sanitary registration of food products, we want to sell our products on the national market . . . we have cattle raising projects and each community receives animals in equal proportions . . . there is more respect for Indigenous peoples, now there are basic services in the small towns . . . . We have made progress during right-wing and leftist governments alike, it was not because of the government, we did it. (personal communication with Guarani Captain, January 14, 2021)

The results obtained by the Guarani regarding the implementation of community projects are comparable to those of their counterparts in Capulálpam de Méndez. Indigenous captains are skilled in prior consultation negotiations and are proud of having ensured that the government fully covers the costs of consultations. Before becoming captain, the respondent disclosed that he had served as a socio-environmental monitor and argued that Ingre has a strong monitoring system in force. In his view, Indigenous members set environmental standards and could make oil companies assume responsibility for the damage they cause. However, he openly expressed his concerns over the negative impacts from sharing their territory with the industry. Moreover, the leader admitted that there is a risk of young socio-environmental monitors being coopted by oil companies.

In March 2015, the Morales government modified prior consultation procedures to be more expeditious and removed the completion of consultations as an impediment for projects to begin (see Supreme Decree 2298, 2015). Later that year, the government approved operations in Natural Protected Areas (see Supreme Decree 2366, 2015). Guarani Captains were able to resist prior consultation counter-reforms and continued to use it in accordance with cultural practices, relying on community assemblies to establish times and procedures for reaching decisions. Still, opposition to extractive operations in Natural Protected Areas remained unarticulated and Guarani leaders were divided between pro-government sectors and more critical voices. The government proceeded with operations despite national and international criticism.

In Ingre, communities have rejected the use of nonconventional seeds as well as dams in order to protect their natural environment. However, hydrocarbon projects are generally approved in Chuquisaca and other regions in El Chaco.[11] Not all captains agree with hydrocarbon operations, but they understand that they cannot refuse these activities (Gustafson 2020; Diaz Arnau n.d.).

Gas Dependence and Repercussions for Indigenous Communities

Despite the progress perceived by some leaders in terms of economic development, civil society organizations and scholarly studies report that extractive revenues have created a heavy dependence among both Indigenous and non-Indigenous populations (Fundacion Jubileo 2018). These organizations report that there is no evidence that Indigenous socio-environmental monitoring on extractive operations has had any impact. Several Indigenous rights and environmental activists denounce the government for using the money negotiated through prior consultation to coopt Indigenous leaders and advance aggressive extractivism. In the view of these sectors, Guarani organizations are now politically weaker, and division between Guarani Captaincies has increased (Ribera 2019).[12]

Furthermore, in a recent report on the impacts of hydrocarbon activities in the department of Tarija, Guarani women report that hydrocarbon operations have more negative than good consequences. In their testimonies, female respondents consider that economic growth only lasts a few years, but environmental and social harms remain for many more: "many women got pregnant by oil employees who lied to them and then abandoned them and their children ...

---

[11] Only the community of Tenteyape, famous for defending the preservation of their culture against the implementation of schools and hospitals in their territories, rejected the oil companies (Mendoza and Terrazas n.d.).

[12] The conflict over the Territorio Indígena y Parque Nacional Isiboro-Sécure (TIPNIS, Indigenous Territory and National Park Isiboro-Sécure) highway in 2012 triggered division in the lowlands. Some Indigenous organizations supported the government whereas others rejected it, invoking environmental and cultural protection (Equipo Nizcor 2012).

there was prostitution which had never happened before, people became lazy, they do not want to work the land anymore, they got used to easy money from working in the companies" (Fundacion Jubileo 2020). Due to these experiences, Guarani leaders from Ingre prohibited oil company employees from interacting with women from the communities, yet they also admit that women work in oil companies and there is a continuous influx of oil workers in Guarani communities (personal communication with Guarani Captain from Ingre, April 2021).

Ecologists criticize Guarani organizations for supporting the government's destructive extractivist policies in exchange for gas revenues (Ribera 2019). This is consistent with the testimonies of Indigenous captains in Ingre who recognize that there are leaders who are tempted by the promise of money. Indigenous respondents agreed that oil companies divide leaders and that bribery, internal conflict, and overlapping leaderships are prevalent (Mendoza and Terrazas n.d.).

Self-Determination as Extractivist Development

The department of Chuquisaca, along with Tarija and Santa Cruz, has the largest hydrocarbon reserves in Bolivia. Since 2012, this department has increased its income due to the gas rents generated by the Caipipendi block. Explorations in gas blocks at Azero and Huacareta in 2014 further increased rents and raised expectations of economic growth (La Razón 2014). Since escaping the *haciendas* (estates), the economic resources most available to Guarani communities, other than NGO support, has come from negotiations with oil companies.

A SLP has enabled the Guarani to hold the government to consultation for any potential project on their land. Unlike other lowland Indigenous groups with few political skills, Guarani organizations can delay oil operations if they are not consulted and compensated in advance. Guarani leaders build upon Indigenous identity and cultural practices to negotiate benefits from oil companies. Community assemblies are used strategically to create Indigenous consensus, make economic demands, and resist government attempts to limit their use of prior consultation.

Nonetheless, gas production has been steadily declining since 2015, and several economic reports warn that poverty reduction could be reverted in the absence of new gas deposit discoveries (Fundacion Jubileo 2018). Economic dependence on extractive revenues prompted the Morales government to authorize hydrocarbon exploration in natural parks in 2015, as well as the use of controversial fracking techniques. This dependence hinders the ability of Guarani organizations to oppose gas extraction or to place limits on oil operations for environmental reasons. The impact of Indigenous monitoring is debatable given the dependence of Indigenous monitors on the companies that pay their salaries.

The Guarani strategy of combining SLP with ER grants these communities partial self-determination, as the economic and cultural dimensions are achieved but the political and legal aspects are reduced. There is increased economic autonomy in the form of locally designed economic projects controlled by Indigenous leaders for the benefit of community members. Cultural values remain a strong guiding force in negotiations with the state and in decisions over the use of ER. However, internal conflicts and oil-related impacts cause serious problems in Guarani societies. Guarani Captains are aware that they are subordinate to state political decisions over gas extraction. Moreover, the continuous influx of oil employees to Indigenous communities, together with Indigenous members joining oil companies and becoming accountable to company norms and interests rather than those of the Guarani, undermine leaders' capacity to make oil employees and community members accountable to Indigenous customary norms.

3.1.3 The Quechua People from Chetilla in Cajamarca, Peru

The Quechua people represent the largest Indigenous group in Peru with a population totaling 5,179,774 (Ministry of Culture of Peru n.d.), concentrated in the highland regions of Cusco, Apurimac, Huacanvelica, Huanuco, Ancash, and Puno. In these regions, Indigenous peoples organize into Peasant Communities (*Comunidades Campesinas*), legally recognized as autonomous bodies entitled to collective property land rights and to use natural resources for their development.[13] Peasant Communities have political, economic, and administrative autonomy and elect their authorities according to their customary norms. Community authorities are accountable to the Community Assembly, the highest decision-making body, where community members deliberate and decide on issues of interest to the community.

The state recognizes these communities as Indigenous with all the rights granted in international and national legislation. Ethnic-centered identities, however, are not overarching in most of the Peruvian Andes and people generally identify as peasants. Traditionally, community leaders have served as intermediaries between their community and the state (Ministry of Culture of Peru n.d.). This type of authority coexists with municipal authorities who are elected through the regular party system, yet a tendency toward municipaliza-tion among Peasant Communities seeking access to state resources has

---

[13] Peasant Communities are recognized in the 1993 constitution, in the General Law of Peasant Communities of 2006, as well as in supplementary legislation.

undermined the authority of traditional leadership (Urrutia 2002). Over the last two decades, peasants have begun to run for municipal seats. However, in order to do this, they are required to form alliances with political parties (Monge 2004). Electoral competition creates division between community members who must choose between the wide array of political parties that emerge during Peru's electoral seasons. Once in office, it is frequent that peasant mayors are subsumed into municipal politics and state development plans.

In addition, another form of community organization exists that has gained importance over the last forty years. In the mid-1970s, various groups of peasants in the Cajamarca region organized patrols to protect community members from local crime (Gitlitz 2013). Subsequently, in the 1980s, when political violence caused by the armed conflict between the Peruvian army and the Shining Path (*Sendero Luiminoso*) gravely affected Quechua societies, this system of community defense, named *Rondas Campesinas* (peasant patrols), assisted the government in defeating the insurgency (Degregori et al. 1996).

In 1993, the new constitution approved by the Fujimori government recognized the power of the *Rondas* to resolve conflicts using customary norms. In 2003, Law 27908 (*Ley de Rondas Campesinas*) granted legal personality to the *Rondas Campesinas* and authorized them to dispense justice and participate in, supervise, and control any type of project or program implemented in their jurisdictions (Articles 1 and 6 of Law 27908). The successful administration of justice by the *Rondas* and their contribution to social peace led the regional government of Cajamarca to support the work of peasant *Ronderos*. Legal training and the implementation of coordination mechanisms between *Ronderos* and state agencies have been established on the understanding that there is no subordination of the peasant justice system to the state but collaboration between the two parties (Digital Platform of the Peruvian Government 2020).

SLP against the Mining Industry

The rural municipality of San Esteban de Chetilla is located in the province of Cajamarca, capital of the Cajamarca region. Chetilla is a Quechua community, politically organized into a municipal council headed by a mayor and five council members elected every four years. The population of Chetilla totals 3,660 (National Institute of Statistics of Peru 2018) and it is the only Indigenous community still inhabiting Cajamarca. Community political organization coexists with municipal authorities (Municipality of Chetilla 2019). Chetilla has the legal status of Peasant Community, accountable to its Community Assembly, together with a strong system of *Rondas Campesinas* that is deeply entrenched in Chetilla's local society due to the effectiveness of the *Ronderos'* administration of justice (Torres-Wong 2019).

Cajamarca is one of the most important mining centers in Peru as it is home to Yanacocha, an open-pit gold mine that has been operating in the region since the 1990s. Mining municipalities in Peru receive a percentage of mining royalties to foster local development (*canon minero*). However, Chetillans oppose mining activities. Environmental disasters attributed to Yanacocha, as well as the numerous conflicts between the company and adjacent communities, account for this rejection (Torres-Wong 2019). Maintaining that water is more valuable than gold, community authorities have remained steadfast in their anti-mining stance, arguing that ecological damages will be greater than the economic development of local communities (Zavaleta Mauricio 2014).[14]

Access to water is critical for Chetilla's agriculturally based economy, as well as for the functioning of its hydroelectric plant. Thus, mining is perceived as a major threat to community survival. In 2003, the Peruvian government authorized several companies to initiate activities in the Colpayoc Mountain, located on Chetilla land. Preliminary studies predicted findings of over 313,000 ounces of gold, using the open-pit exploitation technique (Enlace Minería 2014). However, community members never consented to the operations. Violent confrontations took place between members of the *Ronda Campesina* and mining engineers working in the Colpayoc. In a personal communication, a former member of the municipal council recounts how, without seeking any form of negotiation, hundreds of community members captured the engineers and gathered in the main square. In the presence of community members, leaders burned the engineers' mining equipment, took away their shoes and some clothing, and expelled them from the municipality (personal communication, July 16, 2014, cited by Torres-Wong 2019).

A similar event occurred again in 2009, when the mining company Estrella Gold Peru sent employees to Chetilla to resume exploration activities. Estrella Gold Peru finally withdrew the project in 2013, arguing that the "social costs" were too high and that local conditions needed to change before progressing with mining operations (Enlace Minería 2014). Even today, mining companies have been unable to reinitiate operations. Municipal politicians in Chetilla support the anti-mining stance despite the fact that there is a majority in support of mining in the national government. To secure peasant votes, candidates understand that mining cannot appear on their political agenda (Torres-Wong 2019).

---

[14] Poverty persists in peasant communities in Cajamarca after twenty-two years of gold extraction (National Institute of Statistics of Peru 2018).

Underfunding and the Repercussions for Self-Determination

Low rates of revenue collection together with minimal mining royalties have resulted in a reduced municipal budget, insufficient to cover the population's basic needs. Furthermore, even when Chetillans are united against mining companies, they tend to be divided into different political parties when voting for municipal authorities (for results, see National Office of Electoral Process 2014). Scarce public resources together with increasing divisions over party affiliations prevent both Indigenous and municipal authorities from achieving efficient administration of municipal resources.

In 1995, community authorities organized the *minga* (Quechua for "community work") for the construction of the road that now connects Chetilla to the city of Cajamarca (the main urban center in the region). Chetillans depend on subsistence agriculture, cattle raising, and milk sales. Due to the new road, Cajamarca is now only two hours away by overground transportation, facilitating trade in Chetillan agricultural products and providing some cash income. However, this income is insufficient to improve life in the community. In 2000, a joint effort between community and municipal authorities mobilized Congress representatives to authorize resources for the construction of a hydroelectric plant that now provides electricity to the population at minimum cost (La Rotativa 2013). Nonetheless, Chetilla remains one of the poorest districts of Peru (National Institute of Statistics of Peru 2018). Basic services, such as education and health care, are not adequately covered, and illiteracy and malnutrition are rampant (National Institute of Statistics of Peru 2018). Temporary migration to Cajamarca is common among Chetillans, who leave their hometown for education or temporary jobs to supplement their income.

Tourism has been proposed by various political candidates aspiring to become mayor of Chetilla. In 2018, one candidate, Luis Dilas Mendoza, promised to expand this industry. Natural resources, in the form of water springs, archaeological sites, and distinctive cultural markers such as language, traditional food, clothing, and religious festivities could attract tourists to Chetilla and increase families' income. However, poor road conditions connecting Chetilla with Cajamarca limit access for visitors. In addition, the infrastructure to receive tourists is insufficient, with only two small restaurants and one hotel in the entire district and no travel agencies, tourist guides, or adequate transportation (Montesinos 2018).

When Dilas became mayor, he announced that the government of the province of Cajamarca had approved the construction of the Cumbemayo highway, connecting Chetilla with important archaeological sites. However, according to municipal officials from the city of Cajamarca, the project was indefinitely suspended due to the COVID-19 pandemic (personal communication with council member of the Municipality of Cajamarca, March 10, 2021). In addition, successive political crises in Peru, which have seen four presidents in the last four years, hindered adequate coordination between national and local authorities. This, together with reductions in municipal budgets, has created uncertainty about the availability of the economic resources pledged to Chetilla.

Chetillans continue to make a living from traditional activities which they supplement with government social programs that promote agriculture (Suarez Vasquez 2020). State officials always coordinate with community authorities and the *Rondas* before implementing such programs. Still, neither the *Rondas Campesinas* nor the Community Assembly have the ability to administer public resources. In 2019, the Provincial Municipality of Cajamarca initiated the creation of a special office for *Rondas Campesinas*, to strengthen their capacity to promote development in their communities. This was also interrupted due to the COVID-19 pandemic.

Self-Determination amid Extreme Poverty

Social conflicts and violence over mining projects are common in the Peruvian highlands (OCMAL n.d.). Over the last two decades, Peasant Communities and *Rondas Campesinas* have actively opposed multinational companies, denouncing the social and environmental damage caused by the mining industry (Diez and Ortiz 2013). The Peruvian government has refused to conduct prior consultation in Cajamarca, despite numerous episodes of violent anti-mining mobilization. As it happens, prior consultation is neither necessary nor demanded by Chetillans, as the Peasant Community has built on the justice administration capacities of the *Rondas Campesinas* to prohibit mining.

In Chetilla, strategic SLP allowed community authorities to achieve partial self-determination in its cultural, legal, and political dimensions. Since they began to operate, the *Ronderos* have ensured that the state respects their cultural practices and customary norms to sanction crime and resolve internal conflict. Over the years, the legitimacy acquired by these authorities within their communities enabled them to prohibit unwanted mining projects, contrary to national state decisions. However, the economic dimension of self-determination remains unmet. Community leaders lack the means to carry out new ventures that can eradicate extreme poverty, and their ability to undertake economic projects, such as tourism, is limited by the absence of funding. The community continues to receive social programs and depends on the political will and resources of the national government. Overall, NR prevents Chetillans from achieving full self-determination.

3.1.4 The Maya People from Homún in Yucatan, Mexico

The Maya are the second-largest ethnic group in Latin America after the Quechua, spread across Mexico, Guatemala, Belize, Honduras, and El Salvador. In Mexico, Mayans comprise the second-largest group after the Nahuas, numbering 1,475,575. Mayan speakers inhabit the states of Yucatan, Quintana Roo, Campeche, Chiapas, and Tabasco. In Yucatan, however, where most Mayan communities are found, Indigenous political organization for ethnic-centered demands is uncommon. Some scholars consider the Maya to be "peaceful" in comparison with other groups from Oaxaca, Chiapas, or Michoacan (Mattiace 2013).

The henequen "green gold" industry, prevalent in the region until the mid-twentieth century, transformed Indigenous peasants into wage earners who received a salary from the state company Cordemex. Indigenous communities lost control of their agricultural production and focused most of their political demands on labor rights (Mattiace 2013:227). Nonetheless, more than 65 percent of the population in Yucatan self-identifies as Indigenous even when they do not assert ethnic-centered rights. According to a young Indigenous activist, the Mayan culture permeates life in the Yucatan, and both the language as well as many cultural traditions continue to thrive (personal communication with Indigenous activist, August 2019). However, Mayan communities have remained indifferent to favorable legislation that recognizes their collective rights (Duarte 2013).

Yucatan was the last southern state in Mexico to incorporate pro-Indigenous reforms, which finally occurred in 2011 when the state government approved the Law for the Protection of the Rights of Mayan Communities (*Ley para la Protección de los Derechos de las Comunidades Mayas*). However, various scholars have highlighted that this law did not emerge from Indigenous demands, but rather from federal legislators pressuring the subnational government to regulate Indigenous rights (Mattiace and Llanes Salazar 2015). The new legislation emphasized the most folkloric aspects of Indigenous culture but neglected more substantive affairs, such as Indigenous control of their lands and natural resources (Duarte 2013; Mattiace and Llanes Salazar 2015).

Mayan communities do not use favorable legislation for their political organization and continue to abide by state legal frameworks, exhibiting an ILP. Indigenous authorities are generally absent, and the municipal president is the highest political body at the community level. Participatory and deliberative practices are not common among Indigenous communities (Torres-Mazuera and Recondo 2022). The *ejido* system of collective property of lands is still present but was diluted with the implementation of neoliberal reforms.[15] Currently, the *ejidatarios* (owners of *ejido* lands) operate as private owners

---

[15] The *ejido* is a system of collective land-holding resulting from the 1910 Mexican Revolution.

and are not accountable to the needs and interests of the rest of the community (Torres-Mazuera and Recondo 2022). As a result, neither the *ejido* representatives nor the municipal president serve as a counterweight to federal state decisions that impact Indigenous livelihoods.

Homún is a Mayan municipality inhabited by almost 7,000 people. It is located within the natural protected reserve known as *Anillo de Cenotes* ("the ring of cenotes"), sixty kilometers southeast of the city of Merida (capital of the state of Yucatan). Today, many people from Homún earn their living by working in the ecotourism industry. For years, Homún maintained good relations with state offices and fully complied with state regulations. However, in 2016 the state government authorized the company *Producción Alimentaria y Porcícola* (PAPO) to build a mega pig farm in the municipality. The project triggered opposition from various sectors of Homún which, for the first time, mobilized around the Indigenous right to self-determination and demanded cancellation of the project. A prestigious NGO from Merida supported the Indigenous demands and pursued various legal remedies to finally obtain legal suspension of the project.

Strengthening Indigenous Economy through NER

For the members of Homún, the end of the henequen industry gave rise to an extended period of unemployment. People were forced to migrate to Merida and other parts of Yucatan in search of economic opportunities to support their families. In 2010 a group of community members decided to open *cenotes* for tourism. *Cenotes* are natural pools of crystalline water found either inside caves or in open areas, formed millions of years ago in the Yucatan peninsula as a product of limestone rock erosion. There are approximately 300 *cenotes* in Homún, 13 of which have been opened to visitors (Torres Wong 2022).

Due to the private land regime operating in Homún, the *cenotes* belong to the residents on whose property they are located. Thus, the exploitation of these natural attractions was undertaken through individual initiatives. The National Commission for the Development of Indigenous Peoples (CDI) and the Ministry of Urban Development and the Environment (SEDUMA) supported the *cenote* owners (*cenoteros*), providing them with the economic resources necessary to develop tourist infrastructure or with technical advice to attract national and international tourists. In addition, the CDI helped young people to buy *moto taxis* to transport visitors between the different attractions.[16] While the *cenoteros* are the major beneficiaries of this industry due to the tourist charge for access to the natural pools, new businesses have been developed

---

[16] Moto taxis are motorcycles with wagons attached that can transport up to three passengers.

by young people in the area. In collaboration with *cenoteros*, about 300 young men work as tourist guides and/or in transport services. Small businesses in the form of restaurants, street food vendors, swimming equipment rentals, and lodgings, among others, have also flourished. According to one respondent, Homún has evolved since the exploitation of *cenotes* first began: "there is economic flow" (personal communication with the first *cenotero* of Homún, August 2019). Another commented: "Right now, Homún does not ask the government for anything . . . in four or five years, Homún has managed to self-employ its people" (personal communication with a *cenotero* and restaurant owner of Homun, August 2019).

The decision to open the *cenotes* to tourists implied changes to the cultural patterns of the municipality. The *cenotes* were considered sacred places by the ancient Mayans: "Not everyone could access the *cenotes*, they had to purify themselves, ask for permission". And "our grandparents told us that *cenotes* are special places . . . You have to enter with respect because it is not yours" (interview with Mayan woman and Indigenous rights activist from Merida, August 2019). As a result, many residents were afraid of using the *cenotes* for economic profit. Currently, anyone who pays the entrance fee has access. At the same time, some Mayan traditions regarding the spiritual value of the *cenotes* are being recovered by young tourist guides as foreign visitors show interest in the Indigenous cosmovision.

ILP and Conflict with the Mega Pig Farm

In 2016 the municipal president of Homún authorized changes in land use for the installation of a mega pig farm without informing the population. The *cenoteros* initially believed that a road being built connecting Homún to a nearby lagoon was to promote tourism. When they realized it was not a road, they approached the municipal office for information regarding the type of project being executed, but did not obtain a response. In Merida, the *cenoteros* discovered that PAPO had begun construction of a megaproject aimed at raising 49,000 pigs. The municipal president had authorized the farm without the endorsement of the municipal council. This news generated great concern among *cenoteros* regarding the polluting of their water source.

The company owns more than 100 farms and claims to have created 7,000 jobs from the production of 261,000 tons of pork per year, which is exported to Canada, the United States, Chile, China, Korea, Japan, and Singapore. It has denied causing water pollution as all its facilities have wastewater treatment plants with the most advanced technology (Lliteras 2017). Nevertheless, for many, a project with these propensities represented a threat to the *cenotes* and could negatively impact ecotourism. The *cenoteros* expressed their distrust of the company: "the land [of Yucatan] is very permeable. Everything seeps into the groundwater. Farms make oxidation ponds … there is a lot of corruption, they [state officials] come to inspect, and they [the company] give them their *mocha* [bribe] and they [state officials] say that everything is fine" (personal communication with the first *Cenotero* of Homún, August 2019).

When tensions with PAPO first began, the *cenoteros* did not know how to challenge the municipal decision. The SEDUMA, which had supported the *cenotes* initiative to develop tourism, now supported the implementation of the mega farm, arguing that there was no risk of contamination. A priest from Homún connected the *cenoteros* with *Indignación* (Indignation*)*, a human rights NGO based in Merida. The NGO lawyers were initially skeptical about the case as it appeared to be a business dispute between local entrepreneurs and the government, although *Indignación* finally agreed to take it on. Assisted by NGO members, the *cenoteros* organized into a collective, *Ka'anan Ts'onot* (Mayan voice for guardians of the *cenotes*). By reclaiming their right to self-determination, *Kana'an Ts'onot* set its sights on decisions about community land.

The *cenoteros* argued that the municipal president had not acted in the interests of the people. The farm approval had several flaws, including a deficient environmental impact assessment (Vega 2018). Additionally, the people in Homún were not considered to be Indigenous and there was thus no legal obligation to carry out prior consultation. *Indignación* used a variety of legal remedies to revoke municipal approval of the mega farm. Moreover, legal advisors recommended that the *cenoteros* carry out an Indigenous *autoconsulta* (self-consultation) and convince the people from Homún to vote on the project.

The *autoconsulta* was held on October 8, 2017. Members of *Indignación* were careful to follow the international standards stated by ILO Convention 169 (personal communication with lawyer from *Indignación*, August 2019). State officials from the Ministry of the Environment and Natural Resources (SEMARNAT) and SEDUMA, as well as representatives of PAPO, were invited to the event but did not attend. A public notary certified the validity of the consultation process in the presence of various Indigenous political organizations such as the National Indigenous Congress (CNI) and the Union of Inhabitants of Chablekal in Defense of Land, Territory and Natural Resources, among others. Lawyers from *Indignación*, observers from the United Nations Development Program (UNDP), and the municipal police also attended the process. Of the 4,000 people registered on the municipal electoral roll, a total of 789 attended the event: 732 members voted against the project, 52 voted in favor, and there were 5 spoiled votes. These results were presented to the governor of Yucatan as a sign that the people had voted against the project.

Many residents of Homún remained indifferent to the fight against the mega farm. Some groups with ties to the municipal president supported the project, arguing that it offered job creation, while others saw *Ka'anan Ts'onot* as motivated by the economic interests of their members. Several *cenoteros* had previously occupied the municipal presidency and three of them had received substantial support from the CDI to build their tourist locations, all of which made them vulnerable to charges of corruption. However, as time passed, young tour guides and transport providers, together with their families, began to attend the preparatory meetings for the *autoconsulta*. One female member of Homún recalled that framing the dispute around water quality was decisive in convincing people that the farm was not only a problem for the *cenoteros*, but it would have negative impacts on the entire population (personal communication with female member from *Ka'anan Ts'onot*, August 2019).

In May 2018, a SEDUMA state representative announced that the construction of the mega farm would continue and that despite the legal remedies filed against the farm the project had not been suspended (Diario de Yucatán 2014). At the end of September 2018, the project was inaugurated amid the discontent of the groups that had voted against it. However, shortly after, on October 9, the Judge of the Fourth District of the State of Yucatan declared the definitive suspension of the project. The suspension was in response to the legal resource presented by *Indignación* on behalf of the children of Homún against the municipal president, SEDUMA and the governor of the state for failure to respect their human right to enjoy a healthy environment. The court considered that the evidence presented by the parties showed that the company had not fully guaranteed that water would not be contaminated (Section Amparo, Fourth District of the State of Yucatan [Mexico] 2018, Table V INC1128/2018). The company attempted various legal actions to revoke the sentence, but in November 2020 the administrative courts of Yucatan confirmed the suspension. On July 6, 2021, PAPO filed another legal recourse, arguing that their water treatment plants fulfilled the necessary legal requirements to operate. At the time of writng, the legal dispute remains unresolved (Torres Wong 2022).

Nascent Self-Determination Driven by Economic Growth

The case of Homún illustrates how an Indigenous municipality ruled by ILP and with access to NER was able to increase its levels of self-determination in all dimensions – economic, cultural, legal, and political. Local leaders with *cenotes* on their lands could launch a successful economic model based on individual entrepreneurship and collaboration with state agencies. The *cenoteros* were able to create a waterfall effect that positively impacted the economic situation of many community members. This allowed them to mobilize the support of community members against the mega pig farm. The *autoconsulta*, while lacking legal validity, was a performative exercise of the right to prior consultation in which the people of Homún decided collectively on the future of their lands. Moreover, ecotourism created incentives for a cultural revival as young people strategically began recovering cultural practices to attract tourism.

In spite of this progress, self-determination in Homún is only nascent. Community-centered visions of development are still weak as the ecotourist economy still fails to benefit the majority of residents. As a result, few residents participated in the vote against the company, and those who did participate more actively in the fight against the pig farm were mostly family members of *cenoteros* and young people linked to the ecotourism economy. Decisions on the *cenotes* were not made using customary norms, nor did they include community participation. Most residents remained on the sidelines during the conflict, and many considered that the farm challenged the interests of a handful of landowners.

The *cenoteros* have, until this point, been able to stop the project as a result of the *Indignación* legal strategy which focused on the defense of children's rights. However, the court did not recognize the Indigenous *autoconsulta*, nor did it recognize the Indigenous right to self-determination. The rights of Indigenous peoples remain symbolic in Yucatan, and more substantive outcomes remain to be seen. Nevertheless, the case demonstrates that even in contexts of ILP, NER can have positive impacts on Indigenous self-determination.

3.1.5 The Chontal People from Oxiacaque in Tabasco, Mexico

The southeastern state of Tabasco is home to the *Yokot'anob* or Chontal Indigenous people, spread across the municipalities of Centla, El Centro, Jonuta, Macuspana, and Nacajuca with a total population of 57,296 (Atlas de los Pueblos Indígenas 2015).[17] Chontal communities still preserve their language; however, they have lost most of their distinctive cultural practices and traditions (Vasquez 2000). As in Yucatan, Indigenous ethnic-centered demands are weak. Indigenous communities abide by municipal regulations and elect municipal authorities through the traditional party system. In addition, Tabasco is one of the largest oil producers in Mexico along with Campeche, Tamaulipas, and Veracruz, and most oil perforation takes place on Indigenous land.

Legislation favorable to Indigenous rights was not implemented until 2009 when the law of Indigenous Rights and Cultures was approved by the government of

---

[17] The Chontal belong to the Mayan linguistic family.

Tabasco (Ley de Derechos y Cultura Indígena del Estado de Tabasco, April 25, 2009). As in Yucatan, pro-Indigenous laws did not arise because of Indigenous demands but were adopted to fulfill international norms and Mexico's constitutional provisions. As in most places in Mexico and elsewhere in Latin America, the law authorized Indigenous communities to use their own forms of political organization and customary norms and affirmed that protecting Indigenous cultures was a priority for the state. In 2013, the government of Peña Nieto passed an energy reform that opened the oil industry to private companies. The new legislation included the right to prior consultation for Indigenous communities regarding any effects on their land. In addition, the law mandated that participatory assessments of social impacts, known as EVIS (*Evaluaciones de Impacto Social*) had to be conducted before extraction could proceed. None of these provisions in the legislation, however, had a significant impact on Indigenous peoples in Tabasco.

Chontal communities have been the most impacted by oil operations. In decades of oil activity, Indigenous communities have never been consulted about any project implemented on their land, nor have their environments been adequately restored any time the state oil company, Pemex, or any other company caused damages. Chontal communities live on subsistence agriculture, fishing, and small-scale cattle raising. Thus, degradation of the soil, acid rain, and the contamination of rivers undermine local economies. The rates of unemployment are high among Indigenous members and many struggle to find temporary unskilled employment in the oil industry. Compensations for environmental damage obtained through informal negotiations with Pemex, together with state social programs financed with oil revenues, supplement the fragile economy of most Indigenous communities.

ILP and Oil Extraction

Oxiacaque is a Chontal community with a population of 4,000, which belongs to the municipality of Nacajuca. There is a municipal delegate who only coordinates with the municipal president for the provision of basic services and social programs, as well as an *ejido* Assembly comprising 500 *ejidatarios* (landowners), governed by the Agrarian Law.[18] The *ejido* is responsible for administering land affairs. However, as in Yucatan, there is no collective holding of lands and each *ejidatario* owns their individual plot (*parcela*). Coordination between the *ejido* and the municipal delegate is weak, and each type of authority considers itself to be independent.

Oxiacaque is also home to an oil field known as Campo Sen and has important oil wells located on its land. Even though Oxiacaque is a rural community, the

---

[18] The Agrarian Law was passed following the 1910 Mexican Revolution; it distributed lands to peasants across the country (Guarneros-Meza and Zaremberg 2019).

highways connecting it with the rest of the state are in excellent condition. This infrastructure was built by Pemex and, for Indigenous members, oil employees moving across communities in well-equipped vehicles is a common sight. This contrasts with the office of the municipal delegate that is equipped only with a table and two plastic chairs. The municipal delegate does not receive a budget to implement community projects and depends exclusively on the municipal presidency of Nacajuca. According to one respondent, the lack of public funds defines the relationship between Oxiacaque and the Tabasco government (personal communication with the municipal delegate, May 2018).

Before the oil wells were discovered, community members lived on fishing, agriculture, and poultry farming. According to various community members, a diversity of animals and plants existed that is now difficult to find. No highways connected Oxiacaque with bigger cities such as Paraiso or Villahermosa, and people walked through the forest to get to wherever they needed to go. Older community leaders agree that times were better then as the soil was fertile and, whatever they planted, grew (personal communication with a group of community members, May 2018).

Today, *ejidatarios* are paid rent by Pemex for the occupation of their land; however, there is discontent about this and several members said that the money does not compensate for the damage caused by oil extraction (personal communication with the *ejido* representative, May 2018). Landless community members do not receive rent, and there are no legal mechanisms to compensate communities for environmental damage caused by oil drilling. However, Pemex employees distribute informal compensation to avoid conflict. Oil spills caused by bursting pipelines are common, and rivers and lagoons are contaminated with oil residues which poison fish.[19] Still, respondents described a vicious circle in which it is convenient for some leaders that Pemex continues to pollute the environment as they can then ask for compensation without having to work. This vicious circle is often referred to as Tabasco's "industry of complaint" (*Industria del reclamo*), in which Indigenous peasants are portrayed as "lazy" and using environmental pollution to extort Pemex (Cobos 2017).

Ejido representatives are aware of the environmental standards that oil companies must meet, yet the general perception is that environmental assessments always yield favorable results for Pemex (personal communication with union members, May 2018). Access to fertile land is more

---

[19] This was corroborated by a 1992 report by the National Human Rights Commission in Mexico (*Comisión Nacional de Derechos Humanos* or CNDH) which found that the oil industry had committed several violations of human rights through unrepaired environmental damage and fraudulent compensation to Indigenous communities (Uribe Iniesta 2016).

difficult now, especially for young people. In the past, community members were able to find employment in the oil industry as carpenters, bricklayers, and cleaners, but jobs have become more scarce over time. Unemployed male community members are frequently found at the entrance to Oxiacaque asking for "economic cooperation" from every visitor who comes to the community.

When asked about the participatory mechanisms created by the 2013 legislation that included the voice of Indigenous communities in decisions impacting their land, neither the delegate nor the *ejido* representative had ever heard of the EVIS. Regarding prior consultation, the *ejido* representative said that he had information that Pemex had to consult with the people about what they needed but, as of 2019, this had not occurred.

Conflict over the Explosion of the Terra 123 Oil Well

In October 2013, the Terra 123 oil well located on land near Oxiacaque exploded and burned for over a month causing serious damage to the population's health, local housing, and the environment. People from the community had to be evacuated but many residents decided to stay despite the risks associated with the fire. Pemex was silent about how it was going to mitigate the damages. Oxiacaque members, together with nearby communities, blockaded the highway demanding redress (Torres-Wong 2021).

Several respondents agreed about Pemex's lack of accountability. In the words of the municipal delegate, "the government and Pemex are the same because they work together." One of the few civil society organizations operating in Tabasco, Comité de Derechos Humanos de Tabasco (CODEHUTAB, Commission for Human Rights in Tabasco), supported community members in their fight for justice by providing legal advice during negotiations with the government. In the end, however, the lawyers conceded that little was accomplished as people had given up. To contain the protests, the oil company distributed food, wire fences for peoples' land, farm animals, microcredits, and paid individual compensation to the *ejidatarios* (personal communication with a lawyer from CODEHUTAB, August 2019).

In their testimonies, community members who participated in the blockades explained that they had given up fighting because they lacked support from state authorities and the resources to maintain social mobilization. Community authorities argued that mobilization activities ceased because Pemex made economic commitments, although they believe these were never fulfilled. It is suspected that some leaders and municipal authorities accepted the money paid by the company but kept it and never distributed it to the communities.

Community members have become resigned to the environmental pollution, only requiring fair economic compensation and "development" for the people. There are few signs of any community projects undertaken independently of Pemex resources.

Indigenous Hope, Social Programs, and More Oil

Reflecting on the future, respondents expressed enthusiasm about the then presidential candidate Lopez Obrador (locally known as AMLO), a native of Tabasco, becoming president of Mexico. Several community members commented that they had met Lopez Obrador when he was a young social leader and recalled him with admiration. Interviewees claimed that almost all Chontal members would vote for AMLO, and their hope for change after the 2018 election was evident. According to some, their main objective was to obtain more social programs to improve their economies.

By July 2019, seven months after Lopez Obrador took office, new social programs were already being implemented in Tabasco. In Oxiacaque, the *Sembrando Vida* ("Growing Life") program, aimed at decreasing rural poverty and environmental degradation by increasing sustainable agriculture, provoked different reactions among community members. Some were concerned about the time they would have to wait before seeing results, while others were confident that, over time, peasants would achieve economic improvement based on the growth of their products. One important challenge of the program that was identified by older members was that the younger generations no longer wanted to work in agriculture. Most preferred to find employment with Pemex or in the cities. Several people hoped for the reactivation of the oil industry and the creation of jobs (Torres-Wong 2021).

Along with social programs, state investment in Pemex and oil-related infrastructure has been central to Lopez Obrador's economic agenda. With the discovery of new oil reserves and the construction of the Dos Bocas refinery in Tabasco, the government seeks to reduce dependence on imported gasoline and foster development for Indigenous and non-Indigenous citizens through jobs associated with extractivist infrastructures (Tabasco.gob.mx 2020).[20]

Abundant scientific evidence indicates, however, that hydrocarbon reserves in Mexico are running out and it is unlikely that the country will be able to regain its position among major oil producing countries (Olvera 2020; Buenfil 2005). Environmentalists and scientists have criticized the government's

---

[20] On August 1, 2019, the Congress of Tabasco passed a law known as the Stick Law (*Ley Garrote*) providing that prison sentences would be imposed on protestors who blockade public and private infrastructure. In 2021, the Supreme Court of Mexico declared that prison sentences as provided for in the Stick Law were unconstitutional.

oil-centered policies for being economically and ecologically unsustainable (Ecoosfera 2020). Indigenous communities had never been consulted about whether they approved of oil extraction on their land and with Lopez Obrador in power this has not changed.

Oxiacaque represents the worst-case scenario in terms of Indigenous self-determination. Nationalist discourses in the 1970s – and again today – around oil as the leverage for economic development harms Indigenous possibilities to choose their own development paths. Refusing extraction is impossible, as is developing economic projects outside the realms of extractive rents, informal compensation, or state programs. With the entry of the oil industry, Indigenous peoples were integrated into a nationalist project that undermined their distinctive political institutions, cultural values, and customary norms. Today, there are no deliberative spaces where community members can challenge state decisions that impact their livelihoods. Local authorities do not have a coordination system that enables collective action, nor are there any signs that Lopez Obrador's nationalist government has any interest in promoting these mechanisms.

Oxiacaque members can only hope to obtain fair compensation for all the damages caused by Pemex and to receive state resources distributed through social programs. The hydrocarbon industry remains a priority for the current government. Lopez Obrador strengthened social programs to raise people out of poverty, yet this only represents a continuation of integrationist policies long superseded by international Indigenous rights legislation. The case shows that ER in the context of ILP hinders any form of Indigenous self-determination.

3.1.6 The Awajun People from Atahualpa in Loreto, Peru

Loreto is the largest region of Peru, located in the Amazon basin and home to thirty-two Indigenous ethnic groups. Amazonian Indigenous peoples live in Indigenous communities and are usually part of Indigenous federations that gather together several communities sharing a common territory. Federations comprise subnational political organizations and at the national level; they are part of the Asociación Interétnica de Desarrollo de la Selva Peruana or AIDESEP (Interethnic Association for the Development of the Peruvian Jungle), a political organization representing 109 of these federations. Together with nine other national organizations from the Amazon basin, AIDESEP is part of the international Coordinadora de las Naciones Indígenas de la Cuenca Amazónica or COICA (Umbrella Organization of Indigenous Nations in the Amazon Basin).

Since the 1990s, the Peruvian constitution has recognized Indigenous collective land and the right of Indigenous peoples to organize politically, economically, and administratively, as well as to use their land and resources for their best interests (Article 89 of the Constitution of Peru 1993). In 2003, a new law recognized the longstanding *Rondas Campesinas* and the right to administer justice in Indigenous communities, thereby validating Indigenous use of customary norms to prosecute crime. In 2011, in an emotive ceremony in the city of Bagua, the recently elected Ollanta Humala, who had campaigned in defense of Indigenous rights against extractive companies, approved a law mandating prior consultation for any endeavor attempted on Indigenous lands.

Indigenous organizations at the national and international level have built upon favorable legislation to strengthen their position against the Peruvian government. The conflicts that became more visible in 2000 between Indigenous peoples and the state over extractive projects in the Amazon ended with the 2009 *Baguazo* conflict. Thousands of *Awajun* and *Wampis* members blockaded the *Curva del Diablo* (Devil's curve) highway in the city of Bagua to protest two decrees that sought to privatize community land to promote hydrocarbon extraction. Indigenous protestors claimed that, according to international norms, the government was obligated to consult with Indigenous communities about any measure attempted on their territories. In response, the García government ordered the eviction of protestors, during which thirty-three people were killed, including both police and Indigenous members. International pressure and protest rallies subsequently forced the government to suspend the decrees.

The *Baguazo*, as this conflict became known, was the result of decades of mobilization over respect of Indigenous collective rights. Although the national organization AIDESEP has significant convening and coordinating capacity for collective action, it has poor capacity to improve life in Indigenous territories. Several factors explain this failure: the geographic disconnect of many Amazonian groups and the lack of sufficient resources, mostly provided by international donors, are among the main obstacles to unified action that would benefit the most vulnerable Amazon communities (Flemmer and Schilling-Vacaflor 2016).

The Awajun community of Atahualpa is an example of this disconnect. Located in the region of Loreto in the province of Datem del Marañon, Atahualpa forms part of the rural municipality of Manseriche. Together with nearby communities, it is organized into the Awajun Federation of the Apaga river, or FENARA, formed to protect Indigenous territories and develop their economies; FENARA is also part of the subnational political organization Coordinadora Regional de Pueblos Indígenas or CORPI (Regional Coordinator of Indigenous Peoples), which gathers Indigenous federations from Datem del Marañon.

Amazon communities like Atahualpa are organized into rural municipalities and are often part of supracommunity Indigenous organizations. The lack of affordable river transportation and the long distances that need to be traveled inhibit fluid communication between Atahualpa and the political centers where Indigenous federations and municipal offices operate. As a result, Atahualpa, like many communities in Datem, remains isolated and somehow autonomous from the state.

Recognition of Cultural Rights but without Economic Resources

Strong cultural identities prevail among the Atahualpans, and they preserve their language, political organization, customary norms, and subsistence economies based on fishing, hunting, and gathering (Bártenes 2016). The *Apu* is the traditional authority in Amazon communities, elected through the Community Assembly, the main decision-making body. In Atahualpa, the *Apu* is elected every two years and organizes the political life of the community. In addition, the lieutenant governor (*Teniente Gobernador*), also elected every two years, is responsible for resolving community conflicts. There is also a system of justice administration based on Indigenous paroles or *Rondas Campesinas* for prosecuting local crime and protecting the community.

Like Chetilla, Atahualpa is among the poorest localities in Peru. The community lacks adequate basic services such as health-care centers and schools, and high levels of malnourished children and nursing mothers prevail. The community has a population of 1,000 and is located twenty-four hours away (by boat) from San Lorenzo, the capital city of Datem (the trip may be longer, depending on the river flow). Climate change and the expansion of the mestizo society increasingly limit the natural resources available for Indigenous subsistence. Most Atahualpans have neither the means nor the necessary identity cards to go to the nearest city to receive social program benefits. The few economic resources available take the form of small projects carried out by Catholic missionaries.[21] Indigenous teachers are the only workers who are paid a salary by the state as this is the only professional training available in the province. However, those willing to become teachers must migrate to San Lorenzo (the capital city of Datem) for the training, which is beyond what most families can afford.

For Atahualpa's leaders, it is municipal resources that are most available for implementing community projects. However, Indigenous leaders face many

---

[21] A health center was built with the aid of the NGO Levante in March 2014; however, the absence of health workers willing to work in Atahualpa, and the lack of medicine and electricity, has inhibited its adequate functioning.

obstacles in accessing municipal funding.[22] Datem province has almost always been governed by mestizo mayors.[23] As in the rest of Peru, municipal authorities are elected through the party system, and while the mestizo population is a minority in the area, the Indigenous vote tends to be split between the various ethnic groups seeking municipal office.

In 2014, a group of Indigenous teachers from Atahualpa and nearby communities sought to compete in subnational elections for municipal seats in the province. Indigenous candidates had to form alliances with the non-Indigenous regional movement, MERA, to be able to fulfill Peru's legal requirements and participate in the elections.[24] Indigenous teachers eventually lost the election to non-Indigenous candidates (personal communication with Awajun leader running for mayor in the province, July 8, 2013). This was in part because Indigenous federations from the seven ethnic groups that inhabit Datem del Marañon failed to reach an agreement over which political party to support, and neither AIDESEP nor CORPI endorsed any of the Indigenous candidacies. Indigenous candidates thus joined different political parties, thereby fragmenting the Indigenous vote.

SLP and the Conflict with Repsol

Awajun communities have been at the forefront of Peru's Indigenous movement (Greene 2009), taking a prominent role in anti-oil mobilization in Amazonia. The Awajun from Atahualpa are no exception. Their lands overlap with oil block 109, granted by the Peruvian government to the Repsol oil company without consulting Indigenous communities. The authorities from FENARA, the *Apu*, and Indigenous teachers led the opposition against oil extraction.[25]

In 2008, a confrontation between community members and Repsol employees occurred when the latter attempted to access Atahualpa without permission. Community members seized the ship used by oil employees and sent them back to the capital of the province. However, over the years, community leaders have struggled to maintain a unified position against oil exploitation. Voices critical of anti-oil positions have emerged among some community members seeking to

---

[22] In 2007, an Indigenous leader, Emir Masegkai, was elected as the first provincial mayor of Datem. However, after he left office in 2010 Indigenous candidates have systematically lost elections to mestizo candidates.

[23] With the exception of Emir Mansekai, the first and only Awajun member, who won the first elections in the province in 2005.

[24] MERA is a political movement formed in Iquitos, the capital city of the Loreto region, and named after its founder, Jorge Mera.

[25] "Indigenous teachers known as *maestros billingues* or bilingual teacher, because of their command of Indigenous languages as well as Spanish, represent a new type of Indigenous authority operating as intermediaries between the community and dominant society … they are defenders of collective identities" (Greene 2009:168).

negotiate with the company in the hopes of obtaining jobs and resources. Community leaders were able to silence those voices by appealing to cultural values and the protection of their river and lands. In 2014, Repsol announced its withdrawal from the province due to pervasive conflict with Indigenous communities and the poor results of exploration activities (Saldarriaga 2014). This decision secured Atahualpa's territory and, at the same time, precluded Indigenous access to extractive revenues.

In the elections of 2018, Claudio Wampush, one of the Awajun leaders who had competed in 2014, participated once again and won the municipality of Manseriche, raising enthusiasm among Awajun communities. However, he faced scarce municipal resources and, together with insufficient technical capacity to implement the budget according to municipal bureaucracy, he was prevented from using resources to benefit the communities.

In 2021, FENARA and other Indigenous federations joined the CORPI in their efforts to obtain direct control of state resources designated for the education of Indigenous children (PUINAMUDT 2021). According to Indigenous leaders, the mestizo administration of these funds reproduces discrimination against Indigenous peoples and does not incorporate intercultural principles into education plans. Using ILO Convention 169 to support their case, Indigenous teachers have demanded the right to educate Indigenous communities according to their values and aspirations. The government of Loreto has resisted the idea of having Indigenous teachers administer funds. The dispute is still unresolved and Indigenous federations continue to fight for the resources.

Obtaining assistance from and the cooperation of NGOs is another option Indigenous leaders from Atahualpa pursue; however, access to these resources is competitive, as there are numerous ethnic groups and communities in desperate need of international solidarity. Few communities are able to engage in enduring cooperative relations that can deliver benefits for their members.

Self-Determination by Isolation and State Indifference

Awajun communities have been vocal in the defense of their territories, using their distinctive cultural identities as powerful discursive strategies to demand collective rights. Their participation in the *Baguazo* conflict in 2009 afforded them international fame as radical defenders of their territories against oil extraction. However, the ability of community leaders to implement economic projects that can improve Indigenous living conditions is limited.

Community authorities like the *Apu* or the *Teniente Gobernador* live in conditions of poverty and do not receive any support from the state to perform their functions. Under such conditions, these authorities are incapable of delivering solutions to the most urgent problems that Atahualpans face in their daily lives, creating dissatisfaction with Indigenous institutions and customary norms (personal communication with female member from Atahualpa, January 2022). Political division is on the rise, as Indigenous members affiliate with political parties to compete in elections.

Indigenous candidates who gain municipal office also do not seem to resolve Indigenous problems. Indigenous mayors operating in the remotest areas of the country are generally granted extremely limited budgets to perform their functions. Indigenous political organizations are constantly struggling for economic resources and face resistance from state offices. The Peruvian constitution grants autonomy to Indigenous communities to organize their political and economic affairs and administer justice at the community level. However, as the case of Atahualpa demonstrates, the lack of economic resources (NR) prevents impoverished Indigenous leaders from creating economic alternatives for their people.

As in Chetilla, the case of Atahualpa shows how SLP enables community members to achieve partial self-determination in its cultural, political, and legal dimensions. Atahualpans maintain strong cultural identities and build upon these to defend their land from potential colonizers, such as Repsol and other uninvited visitors. Community work and subsistence activities sustain most members of Atahualpa, even while extreme poverty is rampant. Customary norms still govern the daily life of community members; however, unlike Chetillans, Atahualpans express discontent with the traditional Indigenous system. Arguably, this is due to the lack of state support for Indigenous authorities as they discharge their duties, unlike in Chetilla.

Table 5 offers a typology of self-determination outcomes based on the case studies examined in this Element.

3.2 Discussion of the Cases

Environmentalists, legal advocates, and adherents of the most romantic versions of *Buen Vivir* interrelate the legal protection of Indigenous peoples' rights with the protection of the environment. These positions are consistent with the fact that 40 percent of natural forest and nearly 80 percent of global biodiversity are on Indigenous territories (Scientific American 2021). More recently, international policies have begun to include Indigenous peoples as knowledgeable partners in the mitigation of the impacts of the climate crisis (The Green Initiative and International Labour Organization 2016). In this regard, some scholars have pointed to the need for state policies specifically designed to create partnerships with Indigenous municipalities in order to develop

Table 5. Typology for Self-determination Outcomes

ECONOMIC RESOURCES	FAVORABLE LEGAL FRAMEWORKS	
	SLP	ILP
NER	Capulálpam de Méndez (Full self-determination)	Homún (Nascent self-determination)
ER	Ingre (Partial self-determination)	Oxiacaque (Null self-determination)
NR	Chetilla and Atahualpa (Partial self-determination)	No empirical instances were analyzed Prediction: (Null self-determination)

ecologically sustainable local economies (Carrera-Hernández 2014). Such visions bring together government respect for Indigenous rights, national policies promoting ecologically sustainable development, and the economic resources needed to implement these.

Capulálpam de Méndez in Oaxaca (Mexico) illustrates how Indigenous exercise of self-determination and the protection of the environment can converge. For this community, access to NER stems from partnerships with state agencies seeking to foster sustainable economic activities. A combination of SLP and resources for sustainable economic projects enabled leaders to prohibit mining and create well-being for community members. Through economic alternatives, Indigenous leaders were able to strengthen territorial control, discourage migration and increase the legitimacy of the Indigenous government.

Homún in Yucatán (Mexico) is another case of how NER can create conditions for Indigenous economic growth along with environmental protection. In this case, ILP hindered community unity due to the absence of Indigenous authorities, customary norms, or cultural resistance. This translated into limited capacity to prevent unwanted projects. However, a new economy based on ecotourism created the conditions for young people to revive their culture and oppose projects like the mega farm. The *cenoteros* and NGO members are confident that a reconfiguration of Indigenous government can take place in Homún. The extent to which the tourist model can trigger full self-determination remains to be seen, as well as the ability of *cenoteros* to gain the support of most community members.

Other cases, however, show the inherent risk of idealizing Indigenous relationships with nature. Essentializing Indigenous peoples as radical environmental defenders living in perfect harmony with Mother Earth has proven to be a powerful political discourse to mobilize support from broader sectors of society. However, it may mask the extreme vulnerability in which thousands of Indigenous communities live. Latin American governments still do not allocate sufficient economic resources for the realization of Indigenous peoples' rights, despite the sustained economic growth derived, ironically, from resource exploitation on Indigenous land.

Chetilla and Atahualpa in Peru are examples of this, evincing the poor living conditions of the vast majority of rural Indigenous peoples. Both communities maintain strong cultural identities and most of their cultural practices still guide community life. The culture unites community members for organizing self-defense, community work, and subsistence activities. In both cases, Indigenous leaders chose not to negotiate with extractive companies. Against constitutional provisions that grant the government the capacity to exploit the subsoil, Indigenous members have drawn upon favorable pro-Indigenous legislation to oppose mining and oil industries. However, even when their environment has been protected, Indigenous authorities are left with little capacity to foster well-being and improve living conditions in their territories.

New territorial threats continue to arise in the form of disease, organized crime, and new forms of extractivism. Atahualpans and Chetillans are particularly vulnerable to these threats due to the lack of resources that would allow their leaders to strengthen Indigenous economies. Peru is heavily dependent on mining revenues and, in the last twenty years, the country has been considered the economic miracle of South America for its impressive economic growth (Justo 2016). Still, it seems that resources for extremely poor Indigenous communities unwilling to compromise their territories for the extractive industry remain restricted. Overall, these two cases illustrate that winning the battle against the extractive industry does not ensure full self-determination for Indigenous communities.

On the other hand, activists' concerns regarding the outcomes of prior consultation and compensation, two rights recognized by international norms (Articles 2 and 15 of ILO Convention 169), reveal the imbalances between economic redistribution and the protection of nature, which extractivist economies produce. Prior consultation and compensatory mechanisms aim to safeguard Indigenous self-determination by preventing impositions on Indigenous communities. However, many Indigenous communities – aware that rejecting the extractive industry is not a real possibility during state-led consultations and that few additional sources of income are available – choose economic bargaining over securing their environments from industrialized resource extraction.

Over the last decade, the Guarani Captaincy of Ingre (Bolivia), has built an economic system that relies upon compensation and salaries paid by oil companies. With these resources, Indigenous leaders have improved the functioning of their political organization and implemented ecologically sustainable projects in the hope of achieving independence from extractive companies. However, community projects coexist with gas plants, and oil employees pass through Guarani lands. Guarani leaders struggle to enforce community laws *vis-à-vis* the companies. Preventing environmental impacts is also challenging as socio-environmental monitors are paid for by the companies. A permanent tension thus remains between affirming Indigenous political autonomy and self-government and depending on extractive revenue.

The case of Oxiacaque demonstrates that the situation can become even more complicated if Indigenous communities do not develop the capacity to use existing favorable legislation to enforce their rights. Indigenous customary norms, prior consultation, or social impact assessments (EVIS) remain rhetorical in Tabasco. In such cases, Indigenous dependence on extractive revenues can block any form of self-determination. Individual compensation and informal mechanisms of environmental redress only serve to calm discontent and disarticulate collective action. Indigenous voices are not allowed in decision-making over oil extraction, preventing extractive revenues from improving Indigenous life. Even worse, in Oxiacaque extractive resources are tied to social and environmental damage, thereby creating a vicious circle of pollution, complaints, compensation, and impunity.

3.2.1 What the Cases Demonstrate about Each Country

By focusing on two local factors – Indigenous ability to use favorable pro-Indigenous legislation and the types of economic resources flowing into Indigenous territories – I sought to refocus attention on Indigenous communities and their progress in achieving self-determination. In addition, there are important lessons that can be learned about the three countries examined here.

In Mexico, the best- and worst-case scenarios for Indigenous self-determination can be found. Capulálpam de Méndez with SLP and access to NER achieved full self-determination, whereas in Oxiacaque, Indigenous leaders are coopted and unemployment and environmental degradation is rife. This sharp contrast relates in part to the federative organization of the country which allows the thirty-two states relative legal independence. In general, Mexico has progressive laws regarding Indigenous rights, most of which were implemented in the 1990s during the first wave of rights recognition. However, legal benefits are not equally available for Indigenous communities in all thirty-two states. For instance, self-government rights were implemented in Oaxaca in the 1900s, yet Yucatan and Tabasco did not have legislation in this regard until the mid-2000s. This is also the case with respect to the right to prior consultation which has yet to be legally incorporated through a national law. In some cases, Indigenous populations have been able to use it to negotiate resources, such as the Zapoteca population in Juchitán and the Yaqui People in Sonora. However, these procedures are not systematically enforced across the country.

In addition, national economic resources for Indigenous communities are not equally distributed. Since 2002, Mexico has dedicated a specific section of the Expenditure Budget of the Federation to the development of Indigenous peoples. By 2015, the Indigenous budget had increased fivefold, with economic resources for Indigenous development distributed among various branches (Secretaría de Gobernación n.d.). The National Institute for Indigenous Peoples (INPI), formerly the CDI, allocates part of the budget. In 2018, the government approved a National Program for Indigenous Peoples aimed at strengthening local organization, participation, and sustainable development (INPI 2018). However, the economic resources available from these agencies, even when not tied to extractive projects, are competitive and the criteria to distribute them vary according to the specific objectives of each institution. Communities like Capulálpam and Homún benefited from CDI resources, as they were able to demonstrate that they had the capacity and natural environments to attract tourists. However, Oxiacaque, located near oil reserves, has not been as fortunate.

Bolivia has perhaps the most progressive legislation in Latin America regarding Indigenous rights. Indigenous jurisdictions have the right to convert to AIOCs, prior consultations grant veto power to Indigenous communities, and Indigenous rights have had full constitutional recognition since 2009. However, state funding for Indigenous development is tied to extractive revenue. Bolivia's economy is heavily dependent on gas and there are few alternative sources of income that can be distributed directly to Indigenous communities. Accordingly, progressive laws coexist with retrograde economic policies, increasing dependency on commodity exports.

Peru trails in granting economic access to Indigenous peoples. Peruvian laws regulating Indigenous rights emphasize culture, internal organization, and justice administration. Since 2011, a prior consultation law has obliged the government to consult with Indigenous communities about any project on their land. However, unlike Bolivia, Peru's state officials are reluctant to allow Indigenous communities to use prior consultation to negotiate compensation from extractive companies. The Peruvian economy depends on the export of minerals generally found in the central Andes and promotes the expansion of oil and gas extraction in Amazonia – both are regions inhabited by rural Indigenous peoples. The government, together with extractive companies, has created several funds to distribute extractive resources to Indigenous communities. These funds are coadministered by multiple actors (state, corporate, and Indigenous actors) which dilutes the Indigenous voice in resource administration. Unlike Mexico, there is no national budget for Indigenous development and available economic resources for Indigenous communities are usually tied to specific extractive projects. Over the last five years, the Ministry of Culture has developed new instruments to enable Indigenous communities to achieve self-determination (Ministry of Culture of Peru 2016). Indigenous life planning (*Planes de Vida*), as these instruments are known, draw on the experiences of Colombia and Ecuador and aim to increase organizing capacity and the collective construction of development plans among Indigenous communities (Espinoza 2014). It remains to be seen if these instruments will be accompanied by the economic resources needed for their implementation.

Extractivist economies produce multiple dependences. On the one hand, national governments continue to "sell nature" in exchange for profits, thus lacking sufficient incentives to transform their economies (Gudynas 1996). On the other hand, extractive revenues create dependence, as Indigenous communities trade their subsistence activities for a more sustained flow of economic resources. This poses challenges for Indigenous autonomy as well as for the biodiversity that characterizes Indigenous territories. The findings presented here reveal that one effective way in which Indigenous self-determination goals can converge with environmental sustainability is through economic partnerships between state agencies and Indigenous communities. In the absence of these partnerships, Indigenous communities could develop legal skills to take maximum benefit from extractive resources. Yet, the increase in environmental risks that alliances between Indigenous communities and extractivists could engender should not be overlooked, especially in the face of the threats posed by the climate crisis.

4 Conclusion

Multiple international norms such as ILO Convention 169 (1989), the UNDRIP (2007), and the OAS Declaration on the Rights of Indigenous Peoples (2016) widely recognize the Indigenous right to self-determination. Nevertheless, as progressive as legal frameworks might appear, few Indigenous communities enjoy this right and most remain disempowered, impoverished, and increasingly vulnerable to environmental degradation and climate change (Gouritin 2021).

Indigenous struggles against extractive projects are typically framed as demands for self-determination. Accordingly, many studies document that land dispossession, the aggressive exploitation of natural resources, discrimination, and criminalization of Indigenous protest are all intrinsic to extractivist economies (Global Witness 2020; Svampa 2019). Conversely, Latin American governments argue that extractive resources are the most easily available resource that can be used to improve the lives of Indigenous and non-Indigenous citizens. Meanwhile, Indigenous communities remain divided over the acceptance of extractive projects.

This Element has assessed progress in Indigenous self-determination in three countries where extractivist policies are prevalent. The study of six Indigenous communities with contrasting experiences of extractive industries in Bolivia, Peru, and Mexico has shown that existing legal frameworks favorable to Indigenous rights may be helpful in fostering self-determination. Those Indigenous communities capable of using these laws strategically are better positioned to either ban extractive projects or negotiate extractive resources to their benefit. In addition, the comparative case study demonstrates that economic resources, whether from an extractive or another source, are necessary but not sufficient for Indigenous self-determination.

This Element has offered some preliminary hypotheses based on the cases that may be tested in further studies. Indigenous ability to use favorable legal frameworks to their advantage, together with access to nonextractive resources, is a winning combination for both Indigenous self-determination and the environment. The cases also reflect the fundamental importance of culture for rural Indigenous peoples. Community work, collective holding of land, community assemblies, customary norms, history, memories, and beliefs (real or recreated) are all important traditions reflecting the values that hold community members together against assimilationist laws and industries.

In all six cases, Indigenous authorities demonstrated pragmatism but also concern over the environment, regardless of whether or not they had accepted extractive projects. Congruent with environmentalists and Indigenous discourses on *Buen Vivir*, there is an interdependence between Indigenous communities and their natural environments. However, the cases add nuances to our common understanding of this interdependence. They show that relations between Indigenous communities and surrounding natural resources are in permanent flux. Whether Indigenous communities engage in extractivism or not, guaranteeing environmental sustainability is critical to securing the reproduction of Indigenous collective existence. Furthermore, protecting the biodiversity found in Indigenous territories is as much a matter of global interest as it is of social justice.

Self-determination is a daily struggle pursued through different means by Indigenous communities, which are themselves marked by heterogeneity. Indigenous peoples engage in a permanent search for economic resources to implement community projects that can respond to their needs and aspirations. The difficulties of accessing these resources pushes Indigenous leaders into cooperative relations with state agencies or extractive companies, and this may sometimes mean compromising the integrity of their territories. Ideally, Indigenous communities should have the means to achieve self-determination without having to sacrifice their natural environments.

Appendix: Interviews

Interview with environmental activist participating in Indigenous socio-environmental monitoring (Bolivia), December 2020.

Interview with Guarani Captain from Ingre (Bolivia), March 2021.

Interview with *Ejido* representative from Oxiacaque (Mexico), May 2018.

Interview with municipal delegate of Oxiacaque (Mexico), May 2018.

Interview with union members from Oxiacaque (Mexico), May 2018.

Interview with Agrarian Attorney, Oaxaca (Mexico), October 2018.

Interview with member of Natividad community (Mexico), October 2018.

Interview with the Commissariat of Community Goods of Capulálpam de Méndez, Oaxaca (Mexico), October 2018.

Interview with young professional women of Capulálpam de Méndez (Mexico), October 2018.

Interview with a *cenotero* and restaurant owner of Homún (Mexico), August 2019.

Interview with female member from *Ka'anan Ts'onot* (Mexico), August 2019.

Interview with first *cenotero* of Homún (Mexico), August 2019.

Interview with Indigenous activist from *Indignacion* (Mexico), August 2019.

Interview with lawyer from *Indignacion* (Mexico), August 2019.

Interview with lawyer from the NGO CODEHUTAB in Villahermosa, Tabasco (Mexico), August 2019.

Interview with legal anthropologist (Mexico City), January 2022.

Interview with Awajun teacher from Atahualpa and candidate for mayor of Datem del Marañon (Peru), July 2013.

Interview with former Rondero member of Chetilla (Peru), July 2014.

Interview with municipal council member of Chetilla (Peru), July 2014.

Interview with municipal council member of Cajamarca (Peru), March 2021.

Interview with female member from Atahualpa in Datem del Marañon (Peru), January 2022.

Bibliography

Albó, Xavier. (1987). Algunas Pistas antropológicas para un Orden Jurídico Andino. In D. García-Sayan (ed.) *Derechos Humanos y Servicios Legales en el Campo*. Lima: Comisión Andina de Juristas-Comisión Internacional de Juristas, 55–90.

Altmann, Philipp. (2013). El sumak kawsay en el discurso del movimiento indígena ecuatoriano. *Indiana* 30: 283–299.

Anaya, James. (2000). Self-determination as a Collective Human Right under International Law. In P. Aiko and M. Scheinin (eds.) *Operationalizing the Right of Indigenous Peoples to Self-Determination*. Finland: Institute for Human Rights, Åbo Akademi University, 3–18.

Anaya, James. (2010). Statement by Professor James Anaya, Special Rapporteur, on the situation of the human rights and fundamental freedoms of Indigenous people. *Ninth Session of the UN Permanent Forum on Indigenous Issues*, New York, April 22.

Animal Político. (2020). Día Internacional de los Pueblos indígenas: Por COVID se pierden líderes y conocimientos ancestrales. Available at https://cencos .com.mx/2020/08/dia-internacional-de-los-pueblos-indigenas-por-covid-se-pierden-lideres-y-conocimientos-ancestrales/ (last accessed March 22, 2023).

Aquino, Salvador. (2011). La lucha por el control del territorio en Capulálpam: Diferentes maneras acerca de la comprensión del subsuelo, el oro, la plata, la ley y el capital. Available at www.encuentroredtoschiapas.jkopkutik.org/ BIBLIOGRAFIA/MOVIMIENTOS_POLITICA_CULTURA_Y_PODER/ La_lucha_por_el_control_territorio.pdf.

Arce, Moisés. (2014). *Resource Extraction and Protest in Peru*. Pittsburgh, PA: University of Pittsburgh Press.

Arellano-Yanguas, Javier. (2011). *Minería sin fronteras? Conflicto y desarrollo en regiones mineras del Perú*. Lima: Instituto de Estudios Peruanos.

Atlas de los Pueblos Indígenas. (2015). Tabasco. Available at http://atlas.inpi .gob.mx/tabasco-2/ (last accessed March 9, 2023).

Bártenes, Clever. (2016). Ikama Chichame los Lenguajes del Bosque en la Cosmovisión Awajún: Una exploración desde la ecoetnolingüística. Master's dissertation. Cochabamba: Universidad Mayor de San Simon.

Bartra, M. (2013). Los haceres de la sociedad en torno al medio ambiente Capulálpam de Méndez, Sierra Juárez, Oaxaca, México. *Sociedad y Ambiente* 1 (3): 72–88.

Bebbington, Anthony and Jeffrey Bury. (2009). Institutional Challenges for Mining and Sustainability in Peru. *Proceedings of the National Academy of Sciences* 106 (41): 17296–17301.

Blaser, Mario, Harvey A. Feit, and Glenn McRae. (2004). *In the Way of Development: Indigenous Peoples, Life Projects and Globalization.* London: Zed Books.

Bray, David and Leticia Merino. (2004). *Las experiencias de las comunidades forestales en México: Veinticinco años de silvicultura y construcción de empresas forestales comunitarias.* Mexico: Instituto Nacional de Ecología.

Buenfil, Andrés. (2005). El agotamiento de las reservas, más cerca de lo que se piensa: Cuando se acabe el petróleo. *La Jornada*, October 30. Available at www.jornada.com.mx/2005/10/30/mas-andres.html.

Burguete, Araceli. (2011). Municipalización del Gobierno Indígena e Indianización del Gobierno Municipal en América Latina. *Revista Pueblos y Fronteras Digital* 6 (11): 38–88.

Burguete, Araceli. (2013). Constitutional Multiculturalism in Chiapas: Hollow Reforms That Nullify Autonomy Rights. In Todd A. Eisenstadt, Michael S. Danielson, Moises Jaime Corres, and Carlos Sorroza Polo. (2013). *Latin America's Multicultural Movements: The Struggle between Communitarianism, Autonomy, and Human Rights.* New York: Oxford University Press, 40–65.

Capulálpam de Méndez. (2018). *Biocultural Communitarian Protocol of Capulálpam de Méndez.* Available at https://absch.cbd.int/api/v2013/docu ments/4D03DAC0-33C3-0F01-8370-A093EAABCE69/attachments/PCB% 20Capula%CC%81lpam%20de%20Me%CC%81ndez.pdf.

Carrera-Hernández, Ady. (2014). Municipios metropolitianos gobernados por usus y costumbres: El caso de Santa María Atzompa: Modernidad contra tradición? In C. Cadena (ed.) *Instituciones y actores en sociedades heterógeneas, con rasgo pre post y modernidad.* México: El Colegio Mexiquense.

Caurey, Elias. (2015). Asamblea del Pueblo Guarani: Un breve repaso a su historia. Available at www.esfmjuanmisaelsaracho.edu.bo/libros/lgasam blea.pdf.

Cauthin, Ayala Marielle Claudia. (2017). Relaciones Sociales Entre Guaranies y Karai en el Chaco Bolivia. Master's dissertation. Oaxaca: CIESAS.

Centro Amázonico de Antropología Aplicada. (2020). Santiago Manuin Mayán: "Él no está acá, pero quedamos cientos de Santiagos Manuin, para luchar por un Perú intercultural e inclusivo," July 13. Available at www .caaap.org.pe/2020/07/13/santiago-manuin-mayan-el-no-esta-aca-pero-que damos-cientos-de-santiagos-manuin-para-luchar-por-un-peru-intercultural-e-inclusivo/.

Cepal. (2020). *El Impacto del COVID-19 en los pueblos indígenas de América Latina-Abya Yala: Entre la invisibilización y la resistencia colectiva.* Santiago: United Nations.

Cerqueira, Daniel. (2020). Libre determinacion indigena: Algunos apuntes desde el Derecho Internacional. *Justicia en la Américas* [Blog]. Due Process of Law Foundation, August 10. https://dplfblog.com/2020/08/10/libre-determinacion-indigena-algunos-apuntes-desde-el-derecho-internacional/.

Chávez, Onésimo and Esteban Valtierra-Pacheco. (2018). El papel del Consejo de Caracterizados en la gobernanza de los recursos comunales de Capulálpam de Méndez, Oaxaca. *Temas de Ciencia y Tecnología* 22 (64): 20–30.

Cleaver, Frances and Jessica de Koning. (2015). Furthering Critical Institutionalism. *International Journal of the Commons* 9 (1): 1–18. Available at www.jstor.org/stable/26522813.

Cobos, Octavio. (2017). El impacto de la reforma energética sobre las comunidades indígenas yokot'anob en resistencia en el municipaio de Macuspana, Tabasco. Master's dissertation Mexico: Instituto Nacional de Antropología e Historia.

CONAFOR. (2007). *Experiencias de Manejo Foresta Comunitario.* Oaxaca: Secretaria de Medio Ambiente y Recursos Naturales (SEMARNAT).

CONAIE. (2012). Proyecto Político de la CONAIE 2012. Available at https://conaie.org/2015/07/21/proyecto-politico-conaie-2012/ (last accessed February 7, 2022).

Conde, Marta and Philippe Le-Billon. (2017). Why Do Some Communities Resist Mining Projects While Others Do Not? *The Extractive Industries and Society* 4 (3): 681–697. Available at http://dx.doi.org/10.1016/j.exis.2017.04.009.

Cooke, Erik. (2013). Uses of Autonomy: The Evolution of Multicultural Discourse in Bolivian Politics. In Todd Eisenstadt, Mike Danielson, Moisés Bailón Corrés, and Carlos Sorrosa Polo (eds.) *Latin America's Multicultural Movements. The Struggle between Autonomy, Communitarianism and Human Rights.* New York: Oxford University Press, 67–87.

Cornell, Stephen. (2006). Pueblos indígenas, pobreza y autodeterminación en Australia, Nueva Zelanda, Canadá y EE. UU. In Alberto Cimadomore, Robyn Eversole, and John-Andrew McNeish (ed.) *Pueblos indígenas y pobreza.* Buenos Aires: Clacso, 293–323.

Cortés, Martin. (2008). *Movimientos sociales y Estado en Argentina: Entre la autonomía y la institucionalidad: Informe final del concurso: Gobiernos progresistas en la era neoliberal: Estructuras de poder y concepciones sobre el desarrollo en América Latina y el Caribe.* Programa Regional de Becas, CLACSO.

Daes, Erica-Irene. (2000). The Spirit and Letter of the Right to Self-Determination of Indigenous Peoples. In P. Aiko and M. Scheinin (eds.) *Operationalizing the Right of Indigenous Peoples to Self-Determination.* Finland: Institute for Human Rights, Åbo Akademi University, 3–18.

Dashwood, Hevina. (2007). Canadian Mining Companies and Corporate Social Responsibility: Weighing the Impact of Global Norms. *Canadian Journal of Political Science* 40 (1): 129–156.

Degregori, Carlos Ivan, Jose Coronoe, Ponciano Del Pino, and Orin Star. (1996). *Las rondas campesinas y la derrota de Sendero Luminoso.* Lima: Instituto de Estudios Peruano.

Della Porta, Donatella and Michael Keating. 2008. *Approaches and Methodologies in the Social Sciences: A pluralist perspective.* New York: Cambridge University Press.

Diario de Yucatán. (2014). La Seduma: La granja porcícola cumplió la norma, September 22. Available at www.yucatan.com.mx/merida/2018/9/22/la-seduma-la-granja-porcicola-cumplio-la-norma-66641.html.

Diaz Arnau, Oscar (n.d.). *Fermin Flores, ejecutivo de la Capitanía Ingre* [Interview]. Available at https://indigenas.lapublica.org.bo/inao/fermin-flores-ejecutivo-de-la-capitania-del-ingre/.

Díaz Polanco, Héctor. (1997). *Indigenous Peoples in Latin America: The Quest for Self-Determination.* Translated by Lucía Rayas. Boulder, CO: Westview.

Diez, Alejandro and Santiago Ortiz. (2013). Comunidades Campesinas: Nuevos contextos, nuevos procesos. *Anthropologica* 31 (31): 5–14.

Digital Platform of the Peruvian Government. (2020). Fiscales Rondas Campesinas. Available at www.gob.pe/institucion/mpfn/noticias/292752-fiscales-participaron-encapacitacion-a-rondas-campesinas.

Duarte, Ana Rosa. (2013). Las Autonomías de los Pueblos Mayas de Yucatán y su Silencio ante las Políticas de Asimilación y la Legislación de sus Derechos. *Pueblos y Fronteras Digital* 8: 256–281.

Durante, Francesco, Markus Kröger, and William LaFleur. (2021). Extraction and Extractivisms: Definitions and Concepts. In Judith Shapiro and John McNeish (eds.) *Our Extractive Era: Expressions of Violence and Resistance.* London: Routledge, 19–30.

Ecoosfera. (2020). Destrucción Ilegal de Manglares en Mexico (Cortesía de la Refinería Dos Bocas), March 8. Available at https://ecoosfera.com/refineria-dos-bocas-tabasco-manglares-ecocidio-medioambiente/.

Educa. (2020). A 25 años del reconocimiento constitucional de los usos y costumbres en Oaxaca. August 31. Available at https://desinformemonos

.org/a-25-anos-del-reconocimiento-constitucional-de-los-usos-y-costum
bres-en-oaxaca/.

Eisenstadt, Todd A., Michael A. Danielson, Moises Jaime Corres, and Carlos
Sorroza Polo. (2013). *Latin America's Multicultural Movements: The
Struggle between Communitarianism, Autonomy, and Human Rights*.
New York: Oxford University Press.

Engel, Karen. (2010). *The Elusive Promise of Indigenous Development: Rights,
Culture, Strategy*. Durham, NC: Duke University Press.

Enlace Minería. (2014). Wild Acre Posterga Proyecto Peruano Colpayoc.
Available at http://enlacemineria.blogspot.com/2014/12/wild-acre-posterga-
proyecto-peruano.htm.

Equipo Nizcor. (2012). Ocho directorios de CIDOB no van a la marcha.
April 23. Available at www.derechos.org/nizkor/bolivia/doc/tipnis404.html
(last accessed February 20, 2023).

Espinoza, Oscar. (2014). Los planes de vida y la política indígena en la
Amazonía Peruana. *Anthropologica* 32 (2): 87–114.

Falleti, Tulia and Thea Riofrancos. (2018). Endogenous Participation:
Strengthening Prior Consultation in Extractive Economies. *World Politics*
70 (1): 86–121.

Figuera Vargas, Sorily and Andrea Ariza Lascarro. (2015). Derecho a la
autodeterminación de los pueblos indígenas en el ordenamiento jurídico
colombiano. *Revista de Estudios Sociales* 53: 65–76. https://doi.org/
10.7440/res53.2015.05.

Flemmer, Riccarda. (2015). Interview about the Irregularities of Prior
Consultations in Peru (Part 2). Online video clip. Available at www.you
tube.com/watch?v=ogMUld2_p2E&t=114s.

Flemmer, Riccarda and Almut Schilling-Vacaflor. (2016). Unfulfilled Promises
of the Consultation Approach: The Limits to Effective Indigenous
Participation in Bolivia's and Peru's Extractive Industries. *Third World
Quarterly* 37 (1): 172–188.

Fuente Directa. (2016), En un año, el OEP acompañó 165 procesos de consultas
previas en minería, October 13. Available at http://fuentedirecta.oep.org.bo/
noticia/en-un-ano-el-oep-acompano-165-procesos-de-consultas-previas-en-
mineria/ (last accessed May 30, 2020).

Fundacion Jubileo. (2018). Impacto Económico que puede genera el sector
Hidrocarburos en Chuquisaca. Serie Debate Público 62. Natural Resource
Governance Institute and Brot.

Fundacion Jubileo. (2020). Mujeres e Hidrocarburos. Serie Debate Público 76.
Available at http://jubileobolivia.com/Publicaciones/Revistas-Especializadas/
Mujeres-e-Hidrocarburos.

Fundar. (2017). Pueblos indígenas y organizaciones de la sociedad civil de México, América Latina y el Caribe se pronuncian sobre la implementación del derecho a la consulta y consentimiento previo, libre e informada, November 22. Available at https://fundar.org.mx/pronuncia miento-pueblos-indigenas-y-organizaciones-de-la-sociedad-civil-de-mex ico-america-latina-y-el-caribe-se-pronuncian-sobre-la-implementacion-del- derecho-a-la-consulta-y-consentimient/.

Gil, Vladimir. (2009). *Aterrizaje Minero: Cultura, Conflicto, Negociaciones y Lecciones para el Desarrollo desde la Minería en Ancash, Perú*. Lima: IEP.

Gitlitz, John. (2013). *Administrando Justicia al margen del Estado: Las rondas campesonas en Cajamarca*. Lima: Instituto de Estudios Peruanos.

Global Witness. (2020). *Defending Tomorrow*. Available at www.globalwit ness.org/en/campaigns/environmental-activists/defending-tomorrow/ (last accessed March 1, 2023).

Gómez Rivera, Magdalena. (2013). Los pueblos indígenas y la razón de Estado en México: Elementos para un balance. *Nueva Antropología* 26 (78). www .scielo.org.mx/scielo.php?script=sci_arttext&pid=S0185-0636201300 0100003.

González, Miguel, Araceli Burguete Cal y Mayor, José Marimán, Pablo Ortiz, and Ritsuko Funaki. (2021). *Autonomías y Autogobierno en la América Diversa*. Ecuador: IWGIA.

Gouritin, Armelle. (2018). *Extractivism and Renewable Energies: Human Rights Violations in the Context of Socio-Environmental Conflicts. Illustration Using Wind Farms in San Dionisio del Mar, Oaxaca*. Mexico City: Heinrich Boll Stiftung.

Gouritin, Armelle. (2021). *Migrantes Climáticos en México*. FLACSO: Ciudad de México.

Gouritin, Armelle and Adriana Aguilar. (2017) La adopción de la Declaración Americana sobre los Derechos de los Pueblos Indígenas: Un análisis crítico desde el punto de vista de los derechos ambientales. *Anuario Mexicano de Derecho Internacional* 17: 306–317.

Graham, Lorie. (2004). Resolving Indigenous Claims for Self-Determination. *Journal of International & Comparative Law* 10: 385.

Greene, Shane. (2009). *Customizing Indigeneity: Paths to a Visionary Politcs in Peru*. Stanford, CA: Stanford University Press.

Guarani Autonomous Government Charagua Iyambae. (n.d.). *Estructura de Gobierno de Charagua Lyambae*. Available at www.charagua.gob.bo/estruc tura-de-gobierno-de-charagua-iyambae/.

Guarneros-Meza, Valeria and David Madrigal. (2022). Responsabilidad social empresarial en la minería de Cananea, Sonora, y Cerro de San Pedro, San

Luis Potosí. Desacatos. *Revista De Ciencias Sociales*, 68: 68–85. https:// desacatos.ciesas.edu.mx/index.php/Desacatos/article/view/2487.

Guarneros-Meza, Valeria and Marcela Torres-Wong. (2022). Competing Infrastructures in Local Mining Governance in Mexico. In Jonathan Alderman and Geoff Goodwin (eds.) *The Social and Political Life of Latin American Infrastructure: Meanings, Values, and Competing Visions of the Future*. London: University of London Press, 151–174.

Guarneros-Meza, Valeria and Gisela Zaremberg. (2019). Mapping Violent Conflicts in the Mexican Extractive Industry, October 28. Available at www.opendemocracy.net/en/democraciaabierta/ilustrando-conflictos-en-la-industria-extractiva-de-m%C3%A9xico-en/ (last accessed March 1, 2023).

Gudynas, Eduardo. (1996). *Vendiendo la naturaleza. Impactos ambientales del comercio internacional en América Latina*. La Paz, Bolivia: CLAES, GTZ, and Instituto de Ecología UMSA.

Gudynas, Eduardo. (2012). Estado Compensador y Nuevos Extractivismos: Las ambivalencias del Progresismo Sudamericano. *Nueva Sociedad* 237.

Gudynas, Eduardo. (2014). *Buen Vivir: Sobre Secuestros, Domesticaciones, Rescates y Alternativas*. Quito: Ediciones Yachay.

Gudynas, Eduardo. (2015). *Extractivisms: Ecología, economía y política de un modo de entender el desarrollo y la naturaleza*. Cochabamba: Claes-Cedib.

Guevara, Armando. (2009) *Diversidad y Complejidad Legal: Aproximaciones a la Antropología y a la Historia del Derecho*. Lima: Fondo Editorial PUCP.

Guevara-Gil, Armando and Joseph Thome. (1992). Notes on Legal Pluralism. *Beyond Law* 2 (5): 75–102.

Gustafson, Bret. (2002). Paradoxes of Liberal Indigenism: Indigenous Movements, State Process, and Intercultural Reforms in Bolivia. In David Maybury-Lewis (ed.) *The Politics of Ethnicity: Indigenous Peoples in Latin American States*. Cambridge, MA: Harvard Univesity Press, 267–306.

Gustafsson, Maria-Therese and Almut Schilling-Vacaflor. (2022). Indigenous Peoples and Multiscalar Environmental Governance: The Opening and Closure of Participatory Spaces. *Global Environmental Politics* 22 (2): 70–94.

Hale, Charles. (2002). Does Multiculturalism Menace? Governance, Cultural Rights and the Politics of Identity in Guatemala. *Journal of Latin American Studies* 34: 485–524.

Hale, Charles and Rosamel Millamán. (2007). Puede el multiculturalismo ser una amenaza? Gobernanza, derechos culturales y política de la identidad en Guatemala. In María L. Lagos and Pamela Calla (eds.) *Antropología del*

Estado: Dominación y prácticas contestatarias en América Latina. La Paz, Bolivia: INDH/PNUD, 285–346. Available at www.bivica.org/files/antropo logia-Estado.pdf.

Harder Horst, René. (2020) *History of Indigenous Latin America: Aymara to Zapatistas*. New York: Routledge.

Haslam, Paul. (2004). The Corporate Social Responsibility System in Latin America and the Caribbean. *FOCAL* 4: 1–16.

Haslam, Paul and Pablo Heidrich. (2016). *The Political Economy of Natural Resources and Development: From Neoliberalism to Resource Nationalism*. New York: Routledge.

Healy, Kevin. (1987). *Caciques y Patrones*. Cochabamba: CERES.

Henriksen, John. (2001). Implementation of the Right to Self-Determination of Indigenous Peoples. *Indigenous Affairs* 3: 6–21.

Herrera, Amaya and Maria Elena (2018) Comunidades Indígena Urbanas: Disputa y Negociación por el Reconocimiento. *Andamios* 15 (36): 113–134.

Himley, Mathew (2014). Monitoring the Impacts of Extraction: Science and Participation in the Governance of Mining in Peru. *Environment and Planning* 46 (5): 1069–1087.

Humphreys-Bebbington, Denisse. (2012). Las tensiones Estado-Indigenas debido a la expansion de la industria hidrocarburifere en el Chaco boloviano. In Leonith Hinojosa (ed.) *Gas y Desarrollo: Dinamicas Territoriales Rurales en Tarija-Bolivia*. La Paz: Fundacion Tierra, 132–150.

INPI. (2018). Programa Nacional de los Pueblos Indigenas 2018–2014. Available at www.gob.mx/inpi/es/articulos/programa-nacional-de-los-pueblos-indigenas-2018-2024-mexico-185839?idiom=es.

International Labour Organization. (1989). ILO Convention169. Available at www.ilo.org/dyn/normlex/en/f?p=NORMLEXPUB:12100:0::NO:: P12100_ILO_CODE:C169.

International Labour Organization. (2020). Urgent Action Needed to Tackle Poverty and Inequalities Facing Indigenous Peoples, February 3. Available at www.ilo.org/global/about-the-ilo/newsroom/news/WCMS_735575/lang–en/index.htm (last accessed March 1, 2023).

Justo, Marcelo. (2016). Qué pasó con el milagro económico de Perú? *BBC Mundo*, April 4. Available at www.bbc.com/mundo/noticias/2016/04/160323_america_latina_peru_milagro_economico_elecciones_ppb (last accessed March 1, 2023).

Kymlicka, Will. (1995). *Multicultural Citizenship: A Liberal Theory of Minority Rights*. Oxford: Clarendon Press.

La Razón (2014). Chuquisca busca ser primer productor de Gas, May 25. Available at http://oilproduction.net/details/item/1467-chuquisaca-busca-ser-el-primer-productor-de-gas (last accessed March 9, 2023).

La Rotativa. (2013). Chetilla celebró 13 años de la construcción de su hidroeléctrica, May 31. Available at http://larotativa.pe/chetilla-celebro-13-anos-de-la-construccion-de-su-hidroelectrica/.

Lavinas Picq, Manuela. (2014). Self-Determination as Anti-Extractivism: How Indigenous Resistance Challenges IR. *E-International Relations*, May 21. Available at www.e-ir.info/2014/05/21/self-determination-as-anti-extracti vism-how-indigenous-resistance-challenges-ir/.

Leifsen, Esben, Maria-Therese Gustafsson, Maria Guzman-Gallegos, and Almut Schilling-Vacaflor. (2018). *New Mechanisms of Participation in Extractive Governance: Between Technologies of Governance and Resistance Work*. London: Routledge.

Lightfoot, Sheryl. (2009). Indigenous Global Politics. PhD thesis, University of Minnesota. Available at www.proquest.com/openview/f89e8b6621d128 ce3241bfe912467835/1?pq-origsite=gscholar&cbl=18750.

Lightfoot, Sheryl. (2016). *Global Indigenous Politics. A Subtle Revolution*. New York: Routledge.

Lightfoot, Sheryl (2021). Decolonizing Self-Determination: Huadenosaunee Passports and Negotiated Sovereignty. *European Journal of International Relations* 27 (4): 971–994.

Lliteras, Eduardo. (2017). Se impone el "no" a granja porcícola en Homún. *La Jornada*, October 9. Available at www.lajornadamaya.mx/yucatan/141990/se-impone-el-no-a-granja-porcicola-en-homun.

López Bárcenas, Francisco. (2013). Qué hacemos con los indios? Pueblos indígenas y desarrollo: Entre las políticas gubernamentales y el "buen vivir." *Papeles de Poblaciones* 19 (77): 177–192.

Lopez Flores, Camilo and Gaya Makaran. (2020). Autonomía indígena en disputa: Entre la reconstitución comunitaria y la tutela estatal. La experiencia guaraní de Huacaya en Bolivia. *Revista Crítica de Ciencias Sociais* 121: 49–70.

Lucero, Jose Antonio. (2013). Ambivalent Multiculturalisms: Perversity, Futility and Jeopardy in Latin America. In Todd A. Eisenstadt, Michael S. Danielson, Moises Jaime Bailon Corres, and Carlos Sorroza Polo (eds.) *Latin America's Multicultural Movements: The Struggle Between Communitarianism, Autonomy, and Human Rights*. New York: Oxford University Press, 18–39.

Manos Unidas. (n.d.). Consolidación de la gobernabilidad territorial guaraní mediante la defensa del territorio y el aprovechamiento sostenible de los recursos naturales en Chuquisaca. Available at www.manosunidas.org/proyecto/consolidacion-gobernabilidad-territorial-guarani-mediante-defensa-territorio.

Martí Puig, Salvador (2010). Después de la "década de los pueblos indígenas," qué? El impacto de los movimientos indígenas en las arenas de políticas de América Latina. *Nueva Sociedad* 227. Available at https://nuso.org/articulo/despues-de-la-decada-de-los-pueblos-indigenas-que-el-impacto-de-los-movimientos-indigenas-en-las-arenas-de-politicas-de-america-latina-2/.

Martínez, Juan Carlos. (2006). Los límites del reconocimiento de sistemas normativos y jurisdicción de los pueblos indígenas de Oaxaca. *Alteridades* 16 (31): 49–59.

Martinez, Juan Carlos, Victor Leonel Juan Martinez, and Violeta Hernandez. (2018). *Derechos Indígenas, entre la norma y la praxis*. Berlin: Fundación Konrad Adenauer.

Martinez Novo, Carmen. (2013). The Backlash against Indigenous Rights in Ecuador's Citizen's Revolution. In Todd A. Eisenstadt, Michael S. Danielson, Moises Jaime Bailon Corres, and Carlos Sorroza Polo (eds.) *Latin America's Multicultural Movements: The Struggle between Communitarianism, Autonomy, and Human Rights*. New York: Oxford University Press, 111–131.

Mattiace, Shannan. (2013). Multicultural Reforms for Mexico's Tranquil Indians in Yucatan. In Todd A. Eisenstadt, Michael S. Danielson, Moises Jaime Bailon Corres, and Carlos Sorroza Polo (eds). *Latin America's Multicultural Movements: The Struggle Between Communitarianism, Autonomy, and Human Rights*. New York: Oxford University Press, 217–245.

Mattiace, Shannan and Rodrigo Llanes Salazar (2015). Reformas multiculturales para los mayas de Yucatán. *Estudios Sociológicos* 33 (99): 607–632.

Mendez, Elia. (2017). *De relámpagos y recuerdos ... minería y tradición de lucha serrana por lo común*. Mexico City: Universidad de Guadalajara-CIESAS-Jorge Alonso.

Mendoza, Marco and Lorena Terrazas. (n.d.). Indigenous Socio-Environmental Monitoring Experiences in the Council of Guarani Captain of Chuquisaca CCCH.

Merino, Roger. (2020). Rethinking Indigenous Politics: The Unnoticed Struggle for Self-Determination in Peru. *Bulletin of Latin American Research* 39 (4): 513–528. https://doi.org/10.1111/blar.13022.

Merino, Roger. (2022). Extractive Constitutions: Constitutional Change and Development Paths in Latin America. *Law and Development Review* 15(1): 169–200. https://doi.org/10.1515/ldr-2021-0127.

Ministry of Culture of Peru. (2016). Ministerio de Cultura present instrumento de planificación para los pueblos indígenas u originarios, March 21. Available at www.gob.pe/institucion/cultura/noticias/48958-ministerio-de-cultura-presento-instrumento-de-planificacion-para-los-pueblos-indigenas-u-originarios (last accessed March 1, 2023).

Ministry of Culture of Peru. (n.d.). Consulta Previa. Website. http://consultapre via.cultura.gob.pe/.

Modino, Luis. (2020). Santiago Manuin Mayán: "Él no está acá, pero quedamos cientos de Santiagos Manuin, para luchar por un Perú intercultural e inclusivo," July 13. Available at www.caaap.org.pe/2020/07/13/santiago-manuin-mayan-el-no-esta-aca-pero-quedamos-cientos-de-santiagos-manuin-para-luchar-por-un-peru-intercultural-e-inclusivo/ (last accessed March 1, 2023).

Monge, Carlos. (2004). *Las comunidades campesinas y nuevos marcos institu-cionales: In Las comunidades campesinas en el siglo XXI. Situación actual y cambios normativos*. Lima: Allpa.

Montesinos, Yvette. (2018). Potencial para el desarrollo del turismo vivencial en el distrito de Chetilla, Cajamarca. Bachelor's degree dissertation. Cesar Vallero University: Lima. Available at https://repositorio.ucv.edu.pe/bitstream/handle/20.500.12692/29601/Montesinos_MYJ.pdf?sequence=1&isAllowed=y.

Municipal Council for Sustainable Rural Development. (2009). *Plan de Desarrollo Municipal 2009*. Oaxaca: SAGARPA. Available at https://finan zasoaxaca.gob.mx/pdf/inversion_publica/pmds/08_10/247.pdf.

Municipality of Chetilla. (2019). Plan for Citizen Security. Available at https://docplayer.es/188700680-Municipalidad-distrital-de-chetilla-plan-de-seguri dad-ciudadana.html.Municipality of Chetilla. (2020). Institutional Budget. Available at https://leyes.congreso.gob.pe/Documentos/2016_2021/Consejo_Directivo/Documentos_Otras_Instituciones/OFICIO-215-2019-MDCH-A.pdf.

National Institute of Statistics of Peru. (2018). Map of District Poverty. Available at https://cdn.www.gob.pe/uploads/document/file/1237898/RM_121_2020MIDIS.pdf.

National Office of Electoral Process. (2014). Elleciones Regionales y Municipales 2014. Available at www.web.onpe.gob.pe/modElecciones/elecciones/elecciones2014/PRERM2014/Resultados-Ubigeo-Distrital-EM.html (last accessed March 9, 2023).

Ndayambaje, Olivier and Niyonkuru Fulgence. (2017). Self-Determination as Foundation to Indigenous Peoples' Rights. *Journal of Civil & Legal Sciences* 6 (2): 230. https://doi.org/10.4172/2169-0170.1000230.

OAS. (2016). American Declaration on the Rights of Indigenous Peoples. Available at www.oas.org/en/sare/documents/DecAmIND.pdf.

O'Faircheallaigh, Ciaran and Saleem Ali. (2008). *Indigenous Peoples, the Extractive Industries and Corporate Social Responsibility*. Sheffield, UK: Greenleaf Publishing.

Observatory of Participation, Conflict, and the Environment. (n.d.). Website. http://observandoagoliat.com/.

OCMAL. (2014). Defensores buscan articular estrategias de resistencia contra "proyectos de muerte," November 12. Available at www.ocmal.org/defen sores-buscan-articular-estrategias-de-resistencia-contra-proyectos-de-muerte/ (last accessed April 25, 2020).

OCMAL. (n.d.). Conflictos Mineros en América Latina. Availiable at https:// mapa.conflictosmineros.net/ocmal_db-v2/ (last accessed March 21, 2023).

Oliva, Daniel and Diego Blázquez. (2007). *Los derechos humanos ante los desafíos internacionales de la diversidad cultural*. Valencia: Tirant Le Blanch.

Olvera, Dulce. (2020). El petróleo de fácil acceso se acabó: Expertos. Urge transición energética que Pemex ignora, October 6. Available at www.sinem bargo.mx/06-10-2020/3872242.

Pacheco-Vega, Raul. (2006). Ciudadanía ambiental global: Un recorte analítico para el estudio de la sociedad civil transnacional. *Espiral* (Guadalaj.) 12 (35). Available at www.scielo.org.mx/scielo.php?script=sci_arttext&pid=S1665-05652006000100006.

Paredes, Maritza. (2016). Los pueblos indígenas de Perú apenas cuentan con representación política. Interview in *El Pais*, April 8. Available at https:// elpais.com/internacional/2016/04/01/america/1459466433_618341.html.

Partridge, William L. and Jorge E. Uquillas, with Kathryn Johns. (1996). Including the Excluded: Ethnodevelopment in Latin America. Paper presented at the annual World Bank Conference on Development in Latin America and the Caribbean, Bogota, June 30–July 2.

Penfield, Amy. (2019). Extractive Pluralities: The Intersection of Oil Wealth and Informal Gold Mining in Venezuelan Amazonia. In Cecilie Vindal Ødegaard and Juan Javier Rivera Andia (eds), *Indigenous Life Projects and Extractivism: Ethnographies from South America*. Cham: Palgrave Macmillan, 75–94.

Perez Alfonso, Jorge A. (2020). Frenan zapotecos dos proyectos de mineras en Capulálpam de Méndez. *La Jornada*, February 12. Available at www.jor nada.com.mx/2020/02/12/estados/026n1est.

Picq, Manuela. (2014). Self-Determination as Anti-Extractivism: How Indigenous Resistance Challenges World Politics. In Marc Woons and Ku Leuven (eds.) *Restoring Indigenous Self-determination. Theoretical and Practical Approaches*. Bristol, UK: E-International Relations, 19–26.

Picq, Manuela. (2020). Resistance to Extractivism and Megaprojects in Latin America. *Oxford Research Encyclopedia of Politics*. https://doi.org/10.1093/acrefore/9780190228637.013.1742.

Pieck, Sonja. (2006). Opportunities for Trasnational Indigenous Eco-Politics: The Changing Landscape in the New Millennium. *Global Networks* 6 (3): 309–329.

Povinelli, Elizabeth. (2002). *The Cunning of Recognition: Indigenous Alterities and the Making of Australian Multiculturalism*. Durham, NC: Duke University Press.

Poweska, R. (2017). State-Led Extractivism and the Frustration of Indigenous Self-Determined Development: Lessons from Bolivia. *International Journal of Human Rights* 21 (4): 442–463. https://doi.org/10.1080/13642987.2017 .1284446.

PUINAMUDT. (2021). Pueblos Indígenas del Datem del Marañón protestan por educación, November 15. Available at https://observatoriopetrolero.org/ pueblos-indigenas-de-datem-del-maranon-protestan-por-la-educacion/#:~: text=medidas%20de%20protesta.-,PUINAMUDT%2015%2F11%2F2021.,la %20municipalidad%20de%20San%20Lorenzo (last accessed March 2, 2023).

Ramírez-Espinosa, Naayeli and Daniel Cerqueira. (2021). La libre determinación de los pueblos indígenas en México: Experiencias y regulación. Due Process of Las Foundation, Mexico.

Ribera, Marco Octavio. (2015). *Cronica Ambiental 2013–2015*. Available at https://observatorioccdbolivia.files.wordpress.com/2016/01/cronica-ambien tal-2015.pdf.

Ribera, Marco Octavio. (2019). Mapa de Violaciones a los Derechos Humanos de los Pueblos Indígenas. TICCA Bolivia, February 2019. Available at www .iccaconsortium.org/wp-content/uploads/2017/05/MAPA-DH-PI-2019.pdf (last accessed March 9, 2023).

Rodríguez-Garavito, César. (2011). Ethnicity.gov: Global Governance, Indigenous Peoples, and the Right to Prior Consultation in Social Minefields. *Indiana Journal of Global Legal Studies* 18 (1): 263–305.

Saldarriaga, Juan. (2014). Petroleras se retiraron de siente lotes en el último año. *El Comercio*, March 18. Available at https://elcomercio.pe/economia/peru/ petroleras-retiraron-siete-lotes-ano-167783-noticia/.

Scheidel, Arnim, Daniela Del Bene, Juan Liu et al. (2020). Environmental Conflicts and Defenders: A Global Overview. *Global Environmental Change* 63: 102104. https://doi.org/10.1016/j.gloenvcha.2020.102104.

Scheinin, Martin. (2000). The Right to Self-Determination under the Covenant on Civil and Political Rights. In Pekka Aiko and Martin Scheinin (eds.) *Operationalizing the Right of Indigenous Peoples to Self-determination*. Finland: Institute for Human Rights, Åbo Akademi University, 3–18.

Scientific American. (2021). Biodiversity's Greatest Protectors Need Protection, October 1. Available at www.scientificamerican.com/article/bio diversitys-greatest-protectors-need-protection/.

Secretaria de Gobernación. (n.d.). *Analisis del Presupuesto para el Desarrollo Integral de los Pueblos y Comunidades Indigenas.* Available at www.gob .mx/cms/uploads/attachment/file/32221/presupuesto_2_.pdf.

Servindi. (2015). *Santiago Manuin rompe con De Soto.* Available at www .servindi.org/actualidad/125684 (last accessed March 1, 2023).

Servindi. (2020). Panel Virtual: Autonomía, libre determinación y descolonialidad. Facebook page. www.facebook.com/servindinoticias/vid eos/2612853165638485 (last accessed March 2, 2023).

Sieder, Rachel. (2012). The Challenge of Indigenous Legal Systems: Beyond Paradigms of Recognition. *Brown Journal of Word Law* 18 (2): 103–114.

Sieder, Rachel. (2019). Legal Pluralism and Fragmented Sovereignties: Legality And Illegality in Latin America. In Rachel Sieder, Karina Ansolabehere, and Tatiana Alfonso (eds.) *The Handbook of Law and Society in Latin America.* New York: Routledge, 71–85.

Sieder, Rachel and Barrera, Anna. (2017). Legalizing Indigenous Self-Determination: Autonomy and *Buen Vivir* in Latin America. *Journal of Latin American and Caribbean Anthropology* 22 (1): 9–26.

Starr, June and Jane F. Collier. (2018). *History and Power in the Study of Law: New Directions in Legal Anthropology.* Ithaca, NY: Cornell University Press.

Stavenhagen, Rodolfo. (1992). Challenging the Nation-State in Latin America. *Journal of International Affairs* 45 (2): 421–440.

Stavenhagen, Rodolfo. (2007). Informe del Relator Especial sobre la situación de los derechos humanos y las libertades fundamentales de los indígenas, February 27. Available at www.acnur.org/fileadmin/Documentos/BDL/2007/ 4993.pdf?file=fileadmin/Documentos/BDL/2007/4993.

Stavenhagen, Rodolfo. (2010). *Los Pueblos Indígenas: El Debate Necesario.* Buenos Aires: CLACSO.

Stefanoni, Pablo. (2012). Y quién no querría vivir bien? Encrucijadas del proceso de cambio boliviano. *Cuadernos del Pensamiento Crítico Latinoamericano* 49 (5): 1–4. Available at www.jornada.com.mx/2012/05/ 26/cua-pablo.pdf.

Stensrud, Astrid. (2019). Water as Resource and Being: Water Extractivism and Life Projects in Peru. In Cecilie Vindal Ødegaard and Juan Javier Rivera Andia (eds.) *Indigenous Life Projects and Extractivism: Ethnographies from South America.* Cham: Palgrave Macmillan, 143–164.

Suarez Vasquez, W. (2020). Plantación Forestal en Chetilla. Online video clip. www.youtube.com/watch?v=j1RrfXwPXko.

Svampa, Maristella. (2019). *"Las fronteras del neoextractvismo en América Latina." Conflictos socioambientales, giro ecoterritorial y nuevas dependencias.* Guadalajara: Universidad de Guadalajara and CALAS.

Tabasco.gob.mx. (2020). Visitará AMLO Tabasco con apoyo del 93% de los tabasqueños, February 26. Available at https://tabasco.gob.mx/noticias/visi tara-amlo-tabasco-con-apoyo-del-93-de-los-tabasquenos.

Tapia, Luis. (2000). La densidad de la síntesis. In Alvaro García Liner (eds.) *El retorno de la Bolivia plebeya*. La Paz: Muela del Diablo Editores.

Temper, Leah, Daniela del Bene, and Joan Martinez-Alier. (2015). Mapping the Frontiers and Front Lines of Global Environmental Justice: The EJAtlas. *Journal of Political Ecology* 22: 255–278. https://journals.librarypublishing .arizona.edu/jpe/article/id/1932/.

Territorio Indígena y Gobernanza. (n.d.). El Buen Vivir. Website. www.territor ioindigenaygobernanza.com/web/el-buen-vivir/.

The Green Initiative and International Labour Organization. (2016). *Indigenous Peoples and Climate Change: From Victims to Change Agents through Decent Work*. Available at www.ilo.org/global/topics/indigenous-tribal/ WCMS_551189/lang–en/index.htm.

Tomaselli, Alexandra and Claire Wright. (2020). *The Prior Consultation of Indigenous Peoples in Latin America*. London: Routledge.

Torres Solis, Muricio. (2019). Alternativas al Desarrollo en Latinoamérica. *Latinomaerica revista de estudios latinoamericanos* 69. Available at http:// latinoamerica.unam.mx/index.php/latino/article/view/57106/50898.

Torres-Mazuera, Gabriela and David Recondo. (2022). Asambleas agrarias y comunitarias en el sureste mexicano: Claroscuros de la participación colectiva sobre proyectos eólicos. *Desacatos: Revista De Ciencias Sociales* (68): 12–29. Available at https://desacatos.ciesas.edu.mx/index.php/ Desacatos/article/view/2483.

Torres-Wong, Marcela. (2011). Pluralismo legal en la provincia de Datem del Marañon: Entre el discurso étnico y la práctica política. Master's dissertation. Lima: Pontificia Universidad Católica del Peru.

Torres-Wong, Marcela. (2019). *Natural Resources, Extraction and Indigenous Rights in Latin America: Exploring the Boundaries of State-Corporate Crime in Bolivia, Peru and Mexico*. New York: Routledge.

Torres-Wong, M. (2021) Resource Nationalism and the Violation of Indigenous Rights in Mexico's Oil Industry: The case of a Chontal Community in Tabasco. In Journal of White Collar and Corporate Crime, Vol 4 (1).

Torres-Wong, Marcela and Adrian Jimenez-Sandoval. (2022). Indigenous Resource Governance as an Alternative to Mining: Redefining the Boundaries of Indigenous Participation. *The Extractive Industries and Society* 9: 101001. https://doi.org/10.1016/j.exis.2021.101001.

Torres Wong, M. (2022). Mitos y realidades sobre la autoconsulta indígena en Yucatán: el caso del municipio maya de Homún. *Desacatos. Revista De Ciencias Sociales*, (68), 30–49.

United Nations. (2007). United Nations' Declaration on the Rights of Indigenous Peoples. Available at www.un.org/development/desa/indigenous peoples/declaration-on-the-rights-of-indigenous-peoples.html.

Uribe Iniesta, Rodolfo. (2016). *Tiempos y procesos en la constitución de un espacio regional: El caso de Tabasco*. Mexico City: Universidad Nacional Autónoma de México.

Urrutia, Jaime. (2002). Espacio, poder y mercado: Preguntas actuales para una vieja agenda. In Manuel Pulgar-Vidal, Eduardo Zegarra, and Jaime Urrutia (eds.) *Perú: El problema agrario en debate. Sepia IX*. Lima: Sepia, 473–517.

Van Cott, Dona Lee. (2006). Multiculturalism against Neoliberalism in Latin America. In Keith Banting and Will Kymlicka (eds.) *Multiculturalism and the Welfare State*. London: Oxford University Press, 272–296.

Van Cott, Donna Lee. (2010). Indigenous Peoples Politics in Latin America. *Annual Review of Political Science* 13: 385–405.

Vasquez, Marco Antonio. (2000). "Chontales de Tabasco". *Perfiles Indigenas de Mexico*, CIESAS and Centros Públicos CONACYT. Available at www .aacademica.org/salomon.nahmad.sitton/61.pdf.

Vega, Andrea. (2018). Autorizan con irregularidades granja de 49 mil cerdos en reserva de cenotes en Yucatán. *Animal Político*, February 6. Available at www.animalpolitico.com/sociedad/autorizan-irregularidades-mega-granja-49-mil-cerdos-la-reserva-cenotes-homun-yucatan.

Veltmeyer, Henry and James Petras. (2014). *The New Extractivism: A Post-Neoliberal Development Model, or Imperialism of the Twenty-First Century?* London: Zed Books.

Viale, Claudia and Edgardo Cruzado. (2012). *La Distribucion de la Renta de las Industrias Extractivas a los Gobiernos Subnacionales en Ame rica Latina*. Lima: Revenue Watch Institute.

Viteri, Carlos. (2002). Visión indígena del desarrollo en la Amazonía. *Polis: Revista Latinoamericana* 3: 1–6.

Wade, Pete. (1997). *Race and Ethnicity in Latin America*. London: Pluto Press.

World Bank. (2013). Latinoamérica indígena en el siglo XXI. Available at www.bancomundial.org/es/region/lac/brief/indigenous-latin-america-in-the-twenty-first-century-brief-report-page.

Wright, Claire and Alexandra Tomaselli. (2020). *The Prior Consultation of Indigenous Peoples in Latin America; Inside the Implementation Gap*. New York: Routledge.

Yakovleva, Natalia and Diego Vazquez- Brust. (2012). Stakeholder Perspectives on CSR of mining MNCs in Argentina. *Journal of Business Ethics* 106 (2): 191–211.

Yashar, D. (2005). *Contesting Citizenship in Latin America. The Rise of Indigenous Movements and the Postliberal Challenge*. New York: Cambridge University Press.

Zaremberg, Gisela and Alvaro Guzmán. (2019). Aborto, movimientos y femocracias: Un análisis relacional. *Revista Mexicana de Sociología* 81 (1): 145–177.

Zaremberg, Gisela and Marcela Torres-Wong. (2018). Participation on the Edge: Prior Consultation and Extractivism in Latin America. *Journal of Politics in Latin America* 10 (3): 29–58.

Zavaleta, Mauricio. (2014). *La Batalla por los Recursos Naturales*. Lima: Pontificia Universidad Católica del Peru.

Legislation

Hydrocarbon Law 3058 (Bolivia) (May 17, 2005). Available at https://faolex .fao.org/docs/pdf/bol52651.pdf.

Law of Rondas Campesinas 27908 (Peru) (December 17, 2002). Available at www.justiciaviva.org.pe/acceso_justicia/justicia_comunal/1.pdf.

Ley 29785 del Derecho a la Consulta Previa (Peru) (August 31, 2011). Available at www.minem.gob.pe/minem/archivos/Ley%2029785%20Consulta% 20Previa%20pdf.pdf.

Ley de Derechos y Cultural Indígena del Estado de Tabasco (Mexico) (April 25, 2009). Available at www.cndh.org.mx/sites/default/files/doc/Programas/ Indigenas/OtrasNormas/Estatal/Tabasco/Ley_DCITab.pdf.

Ley para la Protección de los Derechos de la Comunidad Maya del Estado de Yucatán (Mexico) (May 3, 2011). Available at https://vlex.com.mx/vid/ley-proteccion-derechos-comunidad-575284250.

Section Amparo. Fourth District of the State of Yucatan (Mexico) (2018). Sentence in the Case of Homun, *Sección Amparos Mesa V INC1128/2018*. Merida City.

Supreme Decree 29103 (Bolivia) (April 23, 2007). Reglamento de monitoreo socio-ambiental en actividades hidrocarburiferas dentro del territorio de los pueblos indigenas originarions y comunidades campesinas. Available at: www.lexivox.org/norms/BO-DS-29103.html.

Supreme Decree 2298 (Bolivia) (March 18, 2015), consulted online at *Portal Jurídico Lexivox Libre*. Available at www.lexivox.org/norms/BO-DS-N2298.xhtml (last accessed March 21, 2023).

Supreme Decree 2366 (Bolivia) (May 20, 2015), consulted online at *Portal Jurídico Lexivox Libre*. Available at www.lexivox.org/norms/BO-DS-N2366.html#:~: text=No%20est%C3%A1%20permitida%20la%20realizaci%C3%B3n,as% C3%AD%20como%20en%20Sitios%20RAMSAR (last accessed March 21, 2023).

Cambridge Elements ☰

Politics and Society in Latin America

Maria Victoria Murillo

Columbia University

Victoria Murillo is Professor of Political Science and International Affairs at Columbia University. She is the author of *Political Competition, Partisanship, and Policymaking in the Reform of Latin American Public Utilities* (Cambridge, 2009). She is also editor of *Carreras Magisteriales, Desempeño Educativo y Sindicatos de Maestros en América Latina* (2003), and co-editor of *Argentine Democracy: the Politics of Institutional Weakness* (2005). She has published in edited volumes as well as in the *American Journal of Political Science*, *World Politics*, and *Comparative Political Studies*, among others.

Tulia G. Falleti

University of Pennsylvania

Tulia G. Falleti is the Class of 1965 Endowed Term Professor of Political Science, Director of the Latin American and Latino Studies Program, and Senior Fellow of the Leonard Davis Institute for Health Economics at the University of Pennsylvania. She received her BA in Sociology from the Universidad de Buenos Aires and her PhD in Political Science from Northwestern University. Falleti is the author of *Decentralization and Subnational Politics in Latin America* (Cambridge University Press, 2010), which earned the Donna Lee Van Cott Award for best book on political institutions from the Latin American Studies Association, and with Santiago Cunial of *Participation in Social Policy: Public Health in Comparative Perspective* (Cambridge University Press, 2018). She is co-editor, with Orfeo Fioretos and Adam Sheingate, of *The Oxford Handbook of Historical Institutionalism* (Oxford University Press, 2016), among other edited books. Her articles on decentralization, federalism, authoritarianism, and qualitative methods have appeared in edited volumes and journals such as the *American Political Science Review*, *Comparative Political Studies*, *Publius*, *Studies in Comparative International Development*, and *Qualitative Sociology*, among others.

Juan Pablo Luna

The Pontifical Catholic University of Chile

Juan Pablo Luna is Professor of Political Science at The Pontifical Catholic University of Chile. He received his BA in Applied Social Sciences from the UCUDAL (Uruguay) and his PhD in Political Science from the University of North Carolina at Chapel Hill. He is the author of *Segmented Representation. Political Party Strategies in Unequal Democracies* (Oxford University Press, 2014), and has co-authored *Latin American Party Systems* (Cambridge University Press, 2010). In 2014, along with Cristobal Rovira, he co-edited *The Resilience of the Latin American Right* (Johns Hopkins University). His work on political representation, state capacity, and organized crime has appeared in the following journals: *Comparative Political Studies*, *Revista de Ciencia Política*, the *Journal of Latin American Studies*, *Latin American Politics and Society*, *Studies in Comparative International Development*, *Política y Gobierno*, *Democratization*, *Perfiles Latinoamericanos*, and the *Journal of Democracy*.

Andrew Schrank

Brown University

Andrew Schrank is the Olive C. Watson Professor of Sociology and International & Public Affairs at Brown University. His articles on business, labor, and the state in Latin America have appeared in the *American Journal of Sociology*, *Comparative Politics*, *Comparative*

Political Studies, Latin American Politics & Society, Social Forces, and World Development, among other journals, and his co-authored book, Root-Cause Regulation: Labor Inspection in Europe and the Americas, is forthcoming at Harvard University Press.

Advisory Board

About the Series

Latin American politics and society are at a crossroads, simultaneously confronting serious challenges and remarkable opportunities that are likely to be shaped by formal institutions and informal practices alike. The Elements series on Politics and Society in Latin America offers multidisciplinary and methodologically pluralist contributions on the most important topics and problems confronted by the region.

Cambridge Elements ≡

Politics and Society in Latin America

A full series listing is available at: www.cambridge.org/PSLT

Printed in the United States
by Baker & Taylor Publisher Services